WHO IS JESUS?

Answers to Your Questions about the Historical Jesus

John Dominic Crossan
Richard G. Watts

Westminster John Knox Press
Louisville, Kentucky

Book design by Sharon Adams

Cover Design by PAZ Design Group

Published by Westminster John Knox Press

This book is printed on acid-free paper that meets the American National Standards Institute Z39.48 standard. ♾

Printed in the United States of America

00 01 02 03 04 05 06 07 08 - 10 9 8 7 6 5 4 3 2

ISBN 0-664-25842-5

Library of Congress Cataloging-in-Publication Data

Crossan, John Dominic.
    Who is Jesus? : answers to your questions about the historical Jesus / John Dominic Crossan, Richard G. Watts.
        p. cm.
    Originally published: New York : HarperCollins, c1996.
    ISBN 0-664-25842-5 (alk. paper)
    1. Jesus Christ—Historicity Miscellanea. I. Watts, Richard G. II. Title.
BT303.2 .C76 1999
232.9′08—dc21   99-41130
                                                                                CIP

Dedicated to the
New Covenant Community
Normal, Illinois

Acknowledgments

We are grateful to Sarah Crossan who organized hundreds of letters to select and edit those used in this book.

We are grateful to members of the New Covenant Community Church of Normal, Illinois, and others organized by Dick Watts to discuss this book in the various stages of its formation: Pat Abell, Jean Bates, Jim Bortell, Jim Boswell, Julia Cisco, Raydean Davis, Joel Erickson, Willemina Esenwein, Colleen Farlee, Lloyd Farlee, Ann Farnsworth, Randy Gibson, Anita Gilmore, Hal Gilmore, Cheri Grizzard, Julie Jarvis, Mike Kelleher, Otta Key, Dorothy Lee, Caryl Lemke, Skip Lemke, Pam Lewis, Dick LeMoine, Merrilee LeMoine, Cynthia Ashbrook Maurer, Elleke Mesdag, Bill Moonan, Ed Nestingen, Laura Pedrick, Gwen Pruyne, Jim Pruyne, Betty Rademacher, David Rademacher, Jim Roderick, Vera Roderick, Jean Rogers, Margaret Rutter, Russ Rutter, Katie Sawyer, Garrett Scott, Sandy Scott, Jody Stewart, Jerry Stone, Judy Stone, Bill Tolone, Kathy Vitek, Lloyd Watkins, Mary Watkins, Charline Watts, Art White, and Mark Wyman.

We are grateful to Kathy Vitek, not only for her participation in that discussion group, but also for her word processing skills used in the development of this book.

Contents

Why This Book?

"Scholar Refutes Jesus Stories." That was the headline to a front-page newspaper story about a speech I recently gave in a Midwestern university town. That headline, and the story that followed, ignited a firestorm of controversy that raged in the Letters to the Editor pages for the next six weeks. Opinions ranged from "His views are so far out that I can't believe he says he's a Christian" to calling my approach "a way of fully appreciating the richness and beauty of the Gospels, in our 20th century context." So which is it? Is my search for the historical Jesus a threat to faith? Or does it help make faith a possibility for modern men and women?

Actually, that headline writer got it wrong. My purpose was to try to *understand* the stories of Jesus, not *refute* them. The title of my speech that evening was simply "What I've Learned from Thirty-Five Years of Searching for the Historical Jesus." And that is also what this book is about. It is an invitation to journey back in time with me to see Jesus in his own setting in the first-century Jewish home-land. But before we begin, let me tell you a bit about myself and how I got involved in this search.

I grew up in small towns in Ireland. In 1950, at the age of sixteen, I entered the Servites, a Roman Catholic monastic order founded in the thirteenth century. That was the century when Saint Thomas Aquinas combined Aristotle's philosophy with Catholic theology, and never worried that one might contradict the other. Reason and revelation, he insisted, were twin gifts from the same God, and could not be in conflict—unless we misunderstood one or both of them.

That same conviction was deeply embedded in my own heart when, after six years of studying philosophy and theology, I was ordained a priest in 1957. My priestly life was spent more in the library than the parish, and included years of advanced study at the Pontifical Biblical Institute in Rome and the French School of Archaeology in Jerusalem. As a priest, I taught in a number of colleges, universities, and seminaries in the Chicago area.

In 1969 I asked for and received permission to leave the priesthood and the Servite Order. I left primarily in order to marry, but also to avoid a conflict of interest between priestly loyalty and scholarly honesty. The official letter of permission from the Vatican was dated July Fourth—which I considered rather appropriate. Did I leave with feelings of resentment and anger toward the Church? No. While I was a monk and a priest, I was quite happy. When I was no longer happy, I left. It was that simple. Some others have been badly hurt in such transitions; I was not.

From those years in that medieval order I have retained three rather medieval gifts. The first is my name: John is my civil name, and Dominic the new name given me when I entered the Servites. The second is a profound conviction that faith and fact, revelation and reason cannot contradict one another, unless the human mind has misunderstood either or both. The third gift is a very great love for Gregorian Chant, which I sang badly enough to ruin whole choirs and for whose survival my departure was probably a public service.

After leaving the priesthood in 1969, I joined the faculty of DePaul University in Chicago, remaining there until my retirement as Professor Emeritus in 1995. Since I have been a religiously controversial figure, that long tenure is a tribute to the courage and integrity for which DePaul has long stood.

When I joined DePaul, I needed to choose a research focus. At the seminary I had been teaching courses on the parables of Jesus and on the resurrection stories, so I decided to concentrate on the historical Jesus. Year after year I researched and published on particular aspects of Jesus as seen in his own historical context. Indeed, I am probably the only scholar in the world who has spent an entire lifetime on the search for the historical Jesus. That, of course, does not necessarily make me right—but it does make my opinions worth considering.

In 1985 I joined with Robert Funk, newly retired from the University of Montana, in founding the Jesus Seminar, a group of scholars interested in questions of historical Jesus research and Christian origins. The Jesus Seminar usually involves some forty or fifty scholars at four-day sessions held twice a year. What has brought us a lot of public attention is that we not only discuss, we *decide*. Suppose, for example, that we are working together on a subject like the "Kingdom of God" sayings attributed to Jesus in the Gospels. After extensive debate, we vote in secret, using colored beads to indicate our views about how likely it is that the particular words actually came from the historical Jesus. A red bead means that the saying "most likely" came from Jesus, a pink bead means "likely," a gray bead means "not likely," and a black bead means "very unlikely." Although such voting has attracted a lot of media attention, there is really nothing unusual about it. For example, you may have in your home a version of the New Testament which often has footnotes to a particular verse, saying something like, "Other ancient authorities read..." That means that a committee of scholars, looking at ancient manuscripts that are different from each other, have voted on which is most authentic—a process much like ours in the Jesus Seminar.

What has made the Jesus Seminar notorious is that *we do our work out in the open, inviting media attention, letting anyone who is interested in on our processes as well as our conclusions.* We do not want to hide our work in scholarly journals, writing only for one another. We want to let the general public know what we are doing, and to invite them to join the dialogue on major issues of Jesus research.

Besides my work with the Jesus Seminar, during the 1980s I continued to publish the results of my own research, basically for other scholars. But then an amazing thing happened. In 1991 I published *The Historical Jesus: The Life of a Mediterranean Jewish Peasant*, a major summary of my research into Jesus' life and work. I assumed that other scholars would read it, and that the general public would never even hear of it. But Peter Steinfels of *The New York Times* mentioned it in a front-page article around Christmastime, and his story was picked up by many other newspapers. By June, to my great surprise, the book was at the top of *Publishers Weekly* religious bestseller list. A briefer version, *Jesus: A Revolutionary Biography*, was on the same top-ten list for eight months in 1994. (It was pushed downwards by the new *Catechism of the Catholic Church*, which proves that God has a sense of humor.) The unexpected popularity of these books shows a deep and widespread public interest in the figure of Jesus.

Which brings us to the question: Why *this* book?

The answer has four parts. First, there is a need for a brief, easily read introduction to basic questions and conclusions of Jesus research for general readers. Not everyone has the background to plow through the sometimes dense thickets of scholarly argument. This book is meant to make sense to you, even if you have never studied the Bible or had a course on Christian origins. I am trying to make the results of a lifetime of scholarship readily available to non-specialists who want to meet the historical Jesus. Second, in recent years I have done nearly a hundred radio talk shows and probably as many newspaper interviews, and from those have learned a lot about the questions that are on people's minds. This book is written in a question-and-answer style, not only to break up the text into bite-sized chunks, but also to give me a chance to answer typical questions. Third, I have received hundreds of letters—from 38 states and 20 foreign countries—from people who have read my books, heard me speak, or read media reviews of my work. This book not only lets me answer them, but also gives you a chance to see what others are thinking and saying. By the way, I expected negative letters; it is the positive ones that surprised me. For each letter that accuses me of betraying the faith, I get four to five others that basically thank me for helping the writers reconnect with the historical Jesus and their Christian faith. Fourth, this book was conceived in an unusual dialogue between a scholar and a parish church. It all started with some twenty-plus people of New Covenant Community, a small church in Normal, Illinois, who were studying one of my earlier books. When the going got rough, their pastor, Dick Watts, suggested to me that we collaborate on a "translation" of my scholarly work into everyday language. This book is the end product of that collaboration. We sent it out in confidence that many will find it helpful, precisely because it has grown out of the struggle of "real people" to reconnect with Jesus by meeting him in the setting of his own first-century world.

Why Not Just Read the Gospels?

For many years I have been looking for such a book [as Jesus: A Revolutionary Biography*], so much of what I knew about Jesus just didn't "ring true" and yet there was always a slight fear that I might be in some way denying a faith instilled in me as a child and certainly entrenched in the early years of religious life. Your book. . . . has reinforced my own belief that growing involves "unlearning" as well as learning and that this can be very positive and even exciting. . . . Rather than diminish my faith and love for Jesus your book has surely strengthened it and opened up a whole new appreciation of what it means to be a follower of his.*
A woman from Massachusetts

You must be a lucky person to get paid to SEARCH, and to be able to SEARCH as part of your everyday life . . . I'm going on age fifty-two having done little SEARCH . . . maybe I should begin a SEARCH that might make my religion somewhat meaningful. I was forced into baptism, forced through a program of much religious indoctrination and sacraments in Catholic schools. . . . I must take some initiative, away from force, and away from the expectations of others, in pursuit of a God other than this GOD of force. . . . What is more important . . . that we search or that we are satisfied with our answers?
A man from Wisconsin

Your book, The Historical Jesus: The Life of a Mediterranean Jewish Peasant, *has been "our" quest this fall ("our" meaning a bunch of pew-piles looking through glasses darkly for any Jesus at all). We feel bonded to you as our guru in absentia.*

A group from North Carolina

Many people believe that religious faith and science are incompatible—the more you know, the less faith you will have. . . . I assume that you are a man of faith. And as someone who was once an orthodox Catholic who would like to have more faith. . . I have read just enough of the Bible to confuse me. . . . [I write to you as someone who seeks plausible explanations for what seem to me confusing and conflicting passages. . . . There are many passages that are troubling to those of us "who are inquisitive enough to ask questions, but perhaps not smart enough to figure out how to reconcile these passages. But, you must have reconciled these passages with your Catholic faith. But, how?

A man from California

There is definitely a need for a religion that is believable by an intelligent contemporary person with a general background in the sciences. There isn't anything out there that is trying to answer that need.

A man from Massachusetts

I thank Crossan and theologians like him for assuming that I have brains and heart enough to mature with my faith, putting away the storybook and childish interpretations that any close, clearheaded reading of the gospels simply cannot, nor, as I believe, intend to sustain. . . . The bottom line is, if my faith cannot withstand intellectual waves and winds, then, as a Christian, what am I doing in the boat anyway?

A woman from Illinois

One thing I do not understand is how can you and other members of the Jesus Seminar vote on what words Jesus actually said.

Is this something you should be voting about? How can you say that some of what the Bible says is true and other things are not?
A woman from Illinois

Why is research on the historical Jesus necessary at all? Don't we already have four biographies of Jesus—Matthew, Mark, Luke, and John? With four separate biographies in front of us, what's the problem?

Actually, the fact that we have four gospels lies at the very heart of our problem. Because as we read particular parables or sayings or stories in several different versions, we can't miss the *disagreements* between them. At first we are tempted to say, "Well, witnesses simply remember the same things differently." But it is clear that, when Matthew and Luke wrote their gospels, they had copies of Mark (the earliest of the New Testament gospels) in front of them. That means that for much of their story of Jesus, Matthew and Luke are not *independent* sources, but *variations* of Mark. It also means that the variations reflect the theologies of the individual gospel writers. In other words, each gospel is a deliberate *interpretation* of Jesus—rather than a biography.

There is a second problem. Those four gospels are not the only ones written about Jesus. Other gospels are found, either hidden within the four we have in the New Testament or discovered outside them. An example of the first sort is the reconstructed document known as Q. That designation comes from the German word "*Quelle*," which means "source." That text is embedded within both Luke and Matthew, in material common to both of them but not present in Mark. Because I think of that source not just as filler, but as a gospel with its own distinctive theology, I will refer to it throughout this book as the *Q Gospel*.

An example of a document found *outside* Matthew, Mark,

Luke, and John is the *Gospel of Thomas*, which was found in Egypt in 1945. It is, in my view, completely independent of the four New Testament gospels. It is also very different from them in its format—in fact, it is much more like the *Q Gospel*. It is basically a collection of the *sayings* of Jesus without any stories of deeds or miracles, or crucifixion or resurrection.

With all of the differences between Matthew, Mark, Luke, and John and with numerous other gospels existing, we have an obvious problem. Each gospel has a particular way of seeing Jesus. How close to the historical facts are they?

Is there any way to get behind the interpretations to see the Jesus who actually lived?

Many scholarly tools are available to help in that task, and many attempts have been made to paint a picture of the historical Jesus. Some of those pictures are persuasive; some are highly imaginative. Clearly, everything depends upon the methods used to uncover the facts about Jesus. Therefore, I want to clarify at the outset my method for reconstructing the historical Jesus.

I liken my method to three giant searchlights coming together on a single object in the night sky. Each one of the searchlights must strike the object at the same place. Since all three of my "searchlights" must intersect at the same point for any of them to be correct, each serves to correct the other two. Where all three intersect I have a high degree of confidence that they are focused on the historical Jesus.

My first searchlight is *cross-cultural study*. This discipline helps me learn as much as I possibly can about the social setting in which Jesus lived. What I do is look at all of the societies across history that are similar to his. I ask, for example, what I can learn about ancient Mediterranean cultures—as distinct, say, from contemporary American culture. How does an agrarian society differ from an industrial society? What can I learn about phenomena we find in the gospel stories—evil spirits, healing, exorcism? What can scholars tell me about societies that, like the one in which Jesus lived, have elites and peasants, colonial subjects and imperial rulers? What in such a society are politics and family, tax and debt, class and gender relations like? The value of this sort of study is that it has no direct connection with the gospel pictures of Jesus and is, therefore, not likely to be skewed for or against him. To take an example: If I am tempted to picture Jesus as a literate, middle class carpenter, cross-cultural study reminds me that no middle class existed in ancient societies and that the peasant class from which he came is largely illiterate. So I am kept from imagining a Jesus who could not possibly have existed at his time and in his situation.

My second searchlight is *historical study* about Greco-Roman and Jewish affairs in Jesus' time. We know a great deal about the situation of the Jewish homeland as a colony of the Roman Empire, ruled either directly by Roman governors or indirectly by the House of Herod. I give special attention to a fifth-century Jewish historian named Josephus, who wrote two separate but overlapping accounts of that period. Jesus lived amid an undercurrent of peasant unrest and agitation in a land where revolution was just waiting for a chance to happen. And so I listen very carefully to what Josephus tells me about protesters and prophets, bandits and messiahs. If I am to get a true picture of Jesus, I must try to imagine the story of peasant unrest that smolders beneath the surface and never gets recorded until it bursts forth openly into rebellion.

The third searchlight is *textual study*. This is the most difficult part of the quest for the historical Jesus. I have already mentioned that textual study involves sifting

through gospels not only within, but also outside of the
New Testament. But it also means that I have to try to distinguish between *three levels* of the literary tradition. At the
first level the tradition retains sayings and happenings that
go back to the historical Jesus. At the second level those
retained materials are developed—for example, by weaving
stories around originally isolated sayings. The third level
involves creating totally new stories and sayings which are
then put in the mouth of Jesus.

If you have ever read a newspaper story about a priceless
old master painting found in somebody's attic, which had
been covered over by later paintings, you have some idea of
what textual study is like. Just as the art museum curator
goes to work with delicate tools and chemicals to try to
remove the overlay and uncover the original masterpiece,
so scholars use a variety of sophisticated methods to get
down through the layers of interpretation to the original
picture of Jesus.

Are you saying that the gospel writers didn't tell the truth?

Sometimes people are shocked at the notion that
Matthew, Mark, Luke, and John might have elaborated
upon actual events or even created stories and sayings about
Jesus from scratch. We need to understand that the first
Christians experienced Jesus as continuing to be present
with them after he died. That sense of continued presence
gave the transmitters of the Jesus tradition a creative freedom. They did not write so much about the Jesus who *was*,
but the Jesus who *is*; not the Jesus who *said*, but the Jesus
that *says*; not the Jesus who *did*, but the Jesus who *does*. So
they were unembarrassed to restate the words and deeds of
Jesus in ways that met the particular needs of their own
times and communities. When, therefore, I talk about getting behind the gospels to the historical Jesus, I am not

denying the value of gospels as they stand. What I am saying is simply that they are neither histories nor biographies, but interpretations for particular times, places, and communities. In order to see the historical Jesus, we need to get behind those interpretations.

One final point about my method. In an effort to paint a picture of the real Jesus, I pay most attention to the earliest layer of tradition—materials dating between the years 30 and 60 of the first century—and to sayings and stories that are found independently in more than one source from those materials. Stories found in only one source of the tradition may, of course, be accurate, but I try to build my picture of Jesus upward from accounts with multiple independent attestations rather than from accounts with only a single independent attestation. That discipline may not guarantee truth but at least makes it more difficult to be inaccurate.

It is very important for me—*to be honest in my search for the historical Jesus*. I have tried to reconstruct the historical Jesus as accurately as possible. It was never my purpose to try to find a Jesus whom I liked or disliked, a Jesus with whom I agreed or disagreed. I do not pretend that I have the final picture of Jesus, but I do offer my reconstruction as an honest one.

I refer those who wish to explore this subject in more detail and would like to know the scholarly evidence upon which my conclusions are based to my earlier books. *The Historical Jesus: The Life of a Mediterranean Jewish Peasant* is the fullest presentation of my argument. *Jesus: A Revolutionary Biography* is a briefer version of that larger volume. My presentation of the original recorded sayings and earliest pictorial images of Jesus is called *The Essential Jesus*. Finally, the roots of anti-Semitism in the gospel story of the death of Jesus are explored in *Who Killed Jesus?*

2

Son of God,
Son of the Virgin Mary?

I was recently released as a bishop in the Church of Jesus Christ of Latter Day Saints. Shortly afterwards I read your book, The Historical Jesus: The Life of a Mediterranean Jewish Peasant. *Thanks for giving me a new insight to the Jesus Christ I love and worship.*

A man from Illinois

[You write] probably for your own glory and monetary gain—certainly not to increase anyone's faith and probably many people who read stuff like that would lose faith and even leave the church. . . . It would seem that anyone with any energy at all would try to do good by working with people when there is so much to be done to bring souls closer to God.

A woman from Florida

I read an article entitled "Scholar Sees Jesus as Revolutionary" in our local newspaper. I was outraged at the statements you made. . . . MANY, MANY born again Christians, along with those Bible scholars who have made intensive studies of the Bible, have a much different picture of our Lord than you have. . . . You state that Christ was an illiterate peasant, for example. Don't you realize that Christ was God in human form . . . the one who created ALL things and that His knowledge did not have to come from university/theological training! He knew, and knows ALL things and such knowledge is far above what you or I or any human could EVER possibly know!

A woman from Indiana

It is the theologians and researchers like yourself who make my Sunday mornings meaningful. After our Sunday sessions, the whole class feels more comfortable about facing the polarized world of fundamentalism. Thank you for your work and the work of the Jesus Seminar. Your research, your interpretations, and your honesty are appreciated.

A woman from Texas

I like your ideas of a wisdom teacher, using Zenlike aphorisms and puzzling parables to challenge social conventions. But there is something exceedingly *wise and metaphysically true in his teachings, if the Scriptures have them correct, that makes me wonder where he got these truths. Could he have been to India as a youth, or under the tutelage of a teacher from India?*

A man from Missouri

Do you dispute the writings and prophecies of the old prophets that the Virgin would be with child and that Bethlehem, the least of the towns of Judah, would bring forth a leader for all the Israelites (my words)? I don't see anyone trying to change the Old Testament or the prophets' writings! I guess this will be called the "Jesus-Bashing" century.

A man from Florida

I understand you recently participated in the Jesus Seminar and it is alleged in a Toronto Star *report that you do not believe in some of the essentials of the Christian faith. . . . I'm afraid we are all a bit late to prove or disprove the authenticity of the Bible—we might just have to accept it by faith, Mr. Crossan! Besides, don't we* need *Jesus to pay for the wages of our sins? WHY do you disbelieve? What possibly could you gain by denying the essentials of the faith?*

A man from Canada

After hearing your interview with Terri Gross on "Fresh Air," I read your book, Jesus: A Revolutionary Biography *and enjoyed it very much. Being raised a Catholic in the Boston area, attending Catholic schools, and being an altar boy, I learned a lot about ordinary venial and mortal sin, the stations of the cross, the crown of thorns, purgatory and hell, but nothing about the life of Jesus and his message of absolute equality. In rejecting all I was taught about virgin births, miracles and the resurrection, I never studied further who and what Jesus was.*

A man from New Hampshire

What do the birth stories in the gospels tell us about the historical Jesus?

By the "historical Jesus," I mean the real person who walked the dusty roads of Galilee, ate and drank, taught about God's Kingdom, was arrested and executed—so far as historical research can uncover him.

But some of the best-known stories about Jesus do not shed any light on him as a historical figure. I refer to the very familiar nativity stories that we read each Christmas—with Mary and Joseph and the infant Jesus at the manger, surrounded by shepherds, wise men, and angels. The stories of Jesus' birth are religious fiction, or parable, if you prefer. As I will try to show, this does not mean that they have no value, but it does mean that they are not to be read as literal historical fact. Rather, they are like overtures introducing a Broadway musical. An overture catches up the various themes that will be heard throughout the musical. Since Matthew and Luke have produced different versions of the Jesus story, their overtures are different, too.

You said that the story of Jesus' birth is "religious fiction." That must come as quite a shock to most Christian believers. How do you find people reacting to that claim?

Well, the responses are really mixed. Sometimes, of course, I get critical and angry letters either to myself or to newspapers and periodicals that publish my views. On the other hand, I often receive comments from people who express gratitude that they don't need to leave their minds outside the church door when they go to worship. They're grateful to know that it's possible to take the Christian message *seriously* without taking it at all points *literally*.

I assure you that I have no interest in being the Grinch who stole Christmas. I have to be honest as a historian in dealing with the facts as I discover them. But my purpose is a positive one: to present the Jesus who appears to us through the disciplines of historical, literary, and cross-cultural studies. My purpose is not to shock or debunk, but to let the Jesus of history be seen as clearly as possible, apart from theologies about him.

You mentioned that Matthew and Luke tell different birth stories. What are the differences?

If you have a nativity set at home that you put out on the table each Christmastime, it probably centers in a manger—a cattle trough filled with straw in which the infant Jesus rests. Perhaps Mary kneels, while Joseph stands nearby. No doubt there are camels in your nativity set belonging to Wise Men who are offering gifts to the infant. There probably also are cows and donkeys and sheep and shepherds. Perhaps above the rude barn in which the manger is placed, a star is set, an angel figure or two in the background.

In our imaginations we have put the features of two gospels together in one scene. Actually, the two birth stories are very, very different. In Luke's story we have the manger, the shepherds, and the angels. In Matthew's story we have the Wise Men, and they come not to a manger, but to a house. Matthew's story goes on to tell about the Wise Men going to King Herod, who seeks to find out where they can find the child born to be a king. Mary, Joseph, and Jesus flee to Egypt to escape the wrath of Herod, who murders the male children two years old and younger around Bethlehem in an effort to destroy the infant savior. These stories in Matthew have no parallel in Luke.

This chart shows some of the major differences between the two stories, where Matthew and Luke have episodes or settings not found in the other:

MATTHEW	**LUKE**
Angel appears to Joseph	John's conception and birth
Wise Men from the East	Angel appears to Mary
Infant Jesus in the house	Worldwide census
Herod massacres infants	Angel choir
Jesus is taken to Egypt	Jesus' circumcision
	Prophecies of Anna and Simeon

But we can say even more. The first of the gospels to be written, Mark, upon which both Matthew and Luke depend, has no birth story at all. That gospel begins with Jesus as a grown man going to the River Jordan to be baptized by John. The earliest writings in the New Testament, the letters of Paul, contain no reference to birth stories. And the Gospel of John, rather than telling such stories, begins with a meditation on Jesus as the Word of God. So birth stories are found only in Matthew and Luke, and they are radically different one from another.

What this means is that we do not have a straightforward history. What we have, rather, is what I have likened to musical overtures; that is, prefaces to separate gospels that catch up some of the major themes of those gospels. They tell us very little about the historical circumstances of Jesus' birth. But they tell us a great deal about Luke's and Matthew's views of Jesus' place in the story of his people.

If these stories are not historical, then what is their point anyway?

I begin with the birth story in Luke's gospel. What you notice right away is that it is really a story of *two* births, that of Jesus but also of John the Baptist.

John, we're told, is born of aged parents who have long given up any hope of having children. This story looks back to great heroes of Israel's past—to Isaac, who was born of Abraham and Sarah when they were long past the years of childbearing, and to Samuel, who was born to Hannah as a direct result of God's intervention in answer to this infertile woman's prayer. So what we have is the miracle of birth despite infertility and/or old age. We're being told that John is in the tradition of the great heroes of Israel's faith. The story is a common one: persons recognized as great are given special birth stories. A marvelous life and death gets, in retrospect, a marvelous conception and birth.

The story of Jesus' conception and birth parallels that of John—but with the purpose of showing that Jesus is greater than John. John may be born of infertile and aged parents, but Jesus is born of a virgin mother. John's birth is publicized among his neighbors, but Jesus' birth is publicized by a multitude of angels. John's name is specially given to his mother and father after his birth, but Jesus' name is given by an angel before his conception. John is presented publicly and announced as a prophet of the Most High; Jesus is presented in the Temple (rather than just in a home), and the aged Simeon and Anna prophesy of his coming greatness. John is described as growing and becoming strong, filled with wisdom and the favor of God—at age twelve he is found in the Temple astonishing teachers with his insight.

So in the story we see Luke's clear purpose: to link John the Baptist to the great heroes of Israel's faith, but also to show that Jesus is far greater than John. Luke's message to his readers is: John is the fulfillment of Israel's past, but the future belongs to Jesus. Matthew has a similar point, but he expresses it in a quite different story.

How exactly is Matthew's story different?

Take a look at the story as Matthew tells it. He also links the birth of Jesus to ancient Jewish traditions—but goes about it in a different way. Whereas Luke linked the birth of John and Jesus to Isaac and Samuel, Matthew draws parallels between Jesus and Moses.

You remember that in the Exodus story, Pharaoh, the ruler of Egypt, tried to exterminate the people of Israel by commanding that sons born to the Hebrews be thrown into the Nile River to drown. Moses was born at that time and was saved when his mother hid him in a basket near the riverbank, where he was found and then raised by Pharaoh's own daughter. In popular versions of the story that were told in Jesus' time, additional details were added. For example, Moses did not just happen to be born after the massacre was ordered; rather, the massacre was ordered specifically to kill Moses. Pharaoh had been warned that a great leader was about to be born to the Israelites, and so deliberately set out to destroy him. Furthermore, while many of the people of Israel divorced their wives in order to avoid having children that would be massacred, the father of Moses deliberately chose to conceive a child with his wife because of a prophecy about the child's future greatness.

As Matthew begins his gospel, he models the Jesus story on the Moses story. The ruler Herod (like Pharaoh) is warned that a savior is to be born and, therefore, sets out to massacre all the children two years old and younger in the region of Bethlehem to get at the promised deliverer. Joseph (like Moses' father) is tempted to divorce his wife, but is told in a dream about the future greatness of the child, and instead stays with Mary. Moses eventually leads his people out of Egypt, but Jesus is rescued from the murderous tyrant, not by fleeing *from* Egypt, but by fleeing *to* Egypt with his mother and father. By so closely paralleling the stories of Moses and Jesus, Matthew sends a powerful message: *Jesus is the new and greater Moses.*

Now we can see what is happening in these birth stories. Though Luke and Matthew created completely different infancy stories, both had the same purpose. Each used the pattern of Israel's past as a way to interpret the present. In the process, each portrayed Jesus as incomparably greater than any of the ancient heroes on whom his story was modeled. And this is because very early in the Church's life, companions of Jesus searched their scriptures in an effort to understand him and make sense of his fate. Already in these "overtures" we see how Christians used the Hebrew scriptures to interpret Jesus' significance. There are many more examples of this process in the gospels.

You're saying that Matthew and Luke tell different stories, yet both of them agree that he is born of a virgin. And you call these stories "religious fiction." Does that mean that you don't believe in the virgin birth?

It's true that both Matthew and Luke agree on the virginal conception of Jesus. But that story is a perfect illustration of the point I have been making about how Christians searched their scriptures to find ways to speak about the significance of Jesus.

In Matthew's story that searching becomes quite explicit. When an angel speaks to Joseph about the son who is to be born to Mary, Matthew specifically adds that "all this took place to fulfill what had been spoken by the Lord through the prophet: 'Look, a virgin shall conceive and bear a son, and they shall name him Emmanuel (which means God is with us.)'"

Look for a moment at the original setting of the prophet's words, which are found in Isaiah 7:14. Over seven hundred years before the time of Jesus, King Ahaz of Judah, threatened by outside forces, was encouraged by Isaiah to put his trust in God. When Ahaz refused to be assured of God's assistance, Isaiah prophesied a message of doom. But his prophecy had nothing whatever to do with conception by a virgin. The word in Hebrew is "*almah*," which refers to a young woman just married but not yet pregnant with her first child. Isaiah says that a young woman is soon to conceive and bear a son; and before that child grows to maturity, the attacking kingdoms and that of Ahaz will lie devastated. God will indeed be Emmanuel, that is, "God is with us," but in judgment, not salvation. Isaiah's prophecy was specifically addressed to people of his own time. Matthew, however, read those ancient words as a prophecy of hope rather than judgment, and he took the term "virgin" to apply not only to the premarried state of the young woman, but to her state even during and after conception.

Unlike Matthew, Luke does not specifically refer to Isaiah's prophecy, though his language is so close to that of Matthew that we must assume he had it in mind.

What's going on? The passage in Isaiah was not a prediction of Jesus, but a message to a king in Isaiah's day. However, by the time the gospels were written, Christians had already been searching their scriptures for any light they might throw on the identity of Jesus. They had already decided that Jesus was God's chosen one. He already had "saving power" for them. They already believed in the significance of the Jesus who had taught and healed among them and then been crucified. What they then did was *to project that faith in him backwards* onto the time of his conception and birth. Not *all* Christians did so, however. Since this story cannot be found anywhere outside the tradition used by Matthew and Luke, we know that not all Christians read the Isaiah passage in the same way.

By the way, when opponents of Christianity heard claims that he had been born of a virgin, they made the obvious rebuttal that he must have been born illegitimately. A pagan philosopher named Celsus, writing near the end of the second century, claims that the illegitimate father was a Roman soldier named Panthera. In that name we perhaps hear a mocking allusion to the word "*parthenos*," the Greek word for the young Hebrew "*almah*" from Isaiah 7:14.

So you're saying that the virgin birth story was not a fulfillment of prophecy, but a fiction based on an ancient prophecy.

Yes, Isaiah did not *predict* Jesus, but Christians did see in Jesus a *fulfillment* of their own prophetic history, and so they had no trouble using ancient traditions as the core of stories about him.

Let me be very clear. I interpret the story of a virginal conception to be a *confession of faith about the significance of Jesus, not a biological statement about Mary's body*. The virgin birth is a symbol of faith in the adult Jesus, projected backward in time onto Jesus as an infant.

The same process was at work in the story of Jesus' birth in Bethlehem.

Both Matthew and Luke agree that Jesus was born in Bethlehem, a village that lies south of Jerusalem in the hills of Judea. But here again we are in the realm not of history, but of religious fiction, and for the same reason. Matthew specifically tells us that Jesus' birth fulfills an ancient prophecy in the book of Micah that a ruler of Israel would come out of Bethlehem. Though Luke does not quote the

passage (Micah 5:2) explicitly, he also sees Jesus as the fulfillment of the hope for a messiah who would come from
the line of David.

An interesting sidelight is that Matthew assumes that
Mary and Joseph had been already living in Bethlehem.
Luke, however, starts his story with Joseph and Mary living
in Nazareth, and so he has to get them to Bethlehem for
the birth. The way he does that is by his famous story about
a decree

> *that went out from Emperor Augustus that all the world
> should be registered. This was the first registration that was
> taken while Quirinius was governor of Syria. All went to
> their own towns to be registered. Joseph also went from the
> town of Nazareth in Galilee to Judea, to the city of David
> called Bethlehem, because he was descended from the house
> and family of David. (Luke 2:1-7)*

However, there are several problems with that story.
First, there never was a worldwide census under the
Emperor Augustus. Second, though there was indeed a
local census when Quirinius was governor of Syria, it came
about ten years *after* the death of Herod the Great—who
was supposedly still ruling when Jesus was born. Third, we
know from taxation decrees in the Roman world that people were usually registered where they were living and
working. They did not go back to their ancestral homes for
registration and then return to their present homes for
work. That would have been then, as today, a bureaucratic
nightmare. It is a little sad to say this, because the story of
the trip to Bethlehem and the birth in a manger is so beautiful and has inspired such a flowering of Western art,
music, and devotion. But the reality is that the journey for
census and tax registration is sacred fiction, a creation of
Luke's imagination in order to get Jesus' parents to
Bethlehem for his birth. Interestingly, in the Gospel of

John, Chapter 7, we find an argument about whether or not Jesus is the Messiah, and some are arguing that he cannot possibly be since the Messiah must come from Bethlehem. Either the author of John had never heard a claim of a Bethlehem birth for Jesus, or, if he had, he didn't believe it.

All this may seem like nit-picking, and in a way it is. What really matters is that beneath these stories lies the conviction that Jesus was God's son and the Davidic Messiah. That expression of Jesus' significance is deeply embedded within all early Christian traditions. But these particular birth stories were known only to some Christian communities and are picturesque ways of expressing the common faith. In these stories, ancient scriptures are the engine that push the story line along.

So is there nothing in the realm of historical fact that we know about the birth and infancy of Jesus?

That would be overstating it a bit. Jesus was probably born a few years before the start of the first century, around the time of the end of Herod the Great's rule. He was born to Joseph and Mary at Nazareth, a tiny hamlet whose population was probably no more than a few hundred people. From Mark 6:3, we know that he had four brothers (James, Joses, Judas, and Simon) and at least two sisters (unnamed). And we know something about the social class into which Jesus was born—a subject which I will return to in the next chapter.

But the significance of the birth stories does not really lie in the historical data that they give us. The meaning of these stories lies elsewhere. Let me try to get at the meaning by telling you another story of a birth in that ancient Mediterranean world.

The Roman historian Suetonius tells this story of the conception of Augustus, Rome's first emperor and its ruler at the time Jesus was born. He only tells it, by the way, at the end of Augustus' biography, along with the marvels and signs that accompanied his death. On the night of his conception, Augustus' mother, Atia, fell asleep in the Temple of Apollo and was impregnated by the god in the form of a snake. Meanwhile, back at home, Augustus' father, Octavius, dreamt that the sun was arising from his wife's womb. Augustus, in other words, was conceived of a divine father and a human mother. And if you think that such stories had no political or social implications but were just imperial propaganda, look at this ancient decree of calendar change in the Roman province of Asia. It is found on marble stelae in all the Asian temples dedicated to Rome and Augustus.

> *Whereas Providence . . . has . . . adorned our lives with the highest good:* Augustus *. . . and has in her beneficence granted us and those who will come after us [a Savior] who has made war to cease and who shall put everything in [peaceful] order . . . with the result that the birthday of our God signalled the beginning of Good News for the world because of him . . . therefore . . .*

and it goes on to decree that the new year shall begin for all the Asian cities on the birthday of Caesar Augustus.

In light of that decree, listen to Luke's story of the angel announcing Jesus' birth. For the moment do not even ask whether or not it is factual. Don't worry about whether or not it happened. Listen to it in the light of the proclamation about Caesar's birthday.

> *And she gave birth to her firstborn son and wrapped him in bands of cloth, and laid him in a manger, because there was no place for them in the inn. In that region there were shepherds living in the fields, keeping watch over their flock by night. Then an angel of the Lord stood before them, and the*

*glory of the Lord shone around them, and they were terri-
fied. But the angel said to them, "Don't be afraid; for
see—I am bringing you* good news *of great joy for* all the
people: *to you is born this day in the city of David a*
Savior, *who is the Messiah, the Lord. This will be a sign
for you: you will find a child wrapped in bands of clothing
and lying in a manger." And suddenly there was with the
angel a multitude of the heavenly host, praising God and
saying, "Glory to God in the highest heaven, and on earth*
peace *among those whom he favors!" (Luke 2:7–14)*

Now we begin to catch a glimpse of the real question
posed by Luke and Matthew. Where is God to be found on
earth? In Augustus the emperor, or in Jesus the peasant?
Take both stories factually and historically or both stories
metaphorically and symbolically, but face their challenge in
either case: where do you find your God—with the powerful, the conqueror, and the oppressor; or the powerless, the
conquered, and the oppressed?

To show that I'm not just imagining this question from a
twentieth-century point of view, let me go back to the
pagan critic, Celsus. He never argued that the virgin birth
was incredible, only that it was incredible for a member of
the lower classes—a Jewish peasant nobody like Jesus.
"What absurdity!" said Celsus. He knew many stories of
the divine births of Greek heroes. His question of Jesus
was: "What have you done by word or deed that is quite so
wonderful as those heroes of old?" What bothered Celsus
was not the claim that Jesus was *divine*, but the claim *Jesus*
was divine. In fact, class snobbery is very close to the root
of his objection to Christianity. He complains that the religion of Jesus took root in the lower classes and spread
mainly among the vulgar and the illiterate. So it is not just
that Dominic Crossan, a twentieth-century scholar, says
that the meaning of these stories lies elsewhere than in
their literal understanding. The ancient critic also knew

that the question was deeper than that, namely, whether or not in a lower class peasant nobody like Jesus, God could be revealed. Who could believe that?

Let me add that I think that if we had Matthew and Luke here today and asked them whether we should read these stories literally, they would say, "But don't you see? You're missing the point!" So it is not enough to say that there was no guiding star, no manger, no Bethlehem, no shepherds, no angels, no virgin birth. All of those negatives are perfectly true, but they are also quite besides the point. They beg the real question, which was then, as now: where do you find the divine revealed on earth—in Caesar or in Jesus? In imperial grandeur or in peasant poverty? In domination and subjugation of others from the top down, or in the empowerment and liberation of others from the bottom up? Those are the questions that get us to the true meaning of the birth stories about Jesus.

If the virginal conception of Jesus is not literally true, are you saying that Jesus is not the Son of God?

Not at all. But I distinguish emphatically between a statement of fact and a statement of faith. To say that Jesus was human or that Jesus came from Nazareth is a statement of fact, which anyone can make. To say that Jesus is divine or that Jesus came from God is a statement of faith, which only Christians can make. That faith declares that we find God present to us especially, particularly, and uniquely in Jesus. But, Jesus as divine or Jesus as God-for-us is about our relationship to Jesus. It is not as if an electronic scan of Jesus' body would reveal anything inhuman or superhuman. The term "divine" asserts a relationship between God, Jesus, and believers.

In answering that last question, did you deliberately avoid using the title Son of God?

Yes, I think so. When the term "son" was emphasized in Jesus' world, it usually referred to the first-born son, and first-born son meant heir. We who call Jesus "Son of God" declare that all divine gifts come to us in and through Jesus. But in our present world, much father/son language appears chauvinistic and exclusive and I do not find it necessary to use it against that contemporary background. But I insist, once again, that to confess Jesus as Son of God has nothing to do with divine interference in Jesus' normal conception from Mary and Joseph. Virginal conception by divine intervention is a parable expressing in fictional narrative what was already believed, namely, the unique relationship between God, Jesus, and Christian believers.

Christianity has always claimed that it is uniquely true because our Jesus was conceived literally and historically by special divine intervention. What happens to that claim if Jesus was not literally and historically conceived of the Virgin Mary by the power of the Holy Spirit?

All faith, like all love, must be experienced as radically particular and absolutely unique. When a man loves a woman, *this* man loves *that* woman. Our humanity is, at its deepest moments and profoundest depths, particular. Imagine this: I wake up tomorrow morning next to my wife and say, "If I had not met you, fallen in love with you, and married you, I would probably have met someone else, fallen in love with her, married her, and be waking up next to her this morning." That is a very imprudent way to start one's day, and yet we know that it is quite true. But once again, our humanity is achieved in particularity. So faith, like love, must be experienced as unique, absolute, irreplaceable. But we must know that others experience their faith as equally unique, absolutely, and irreplaceable. Every religion, Christianity like all others, must be experienced as absolutely unique to the believer. But all religions, Christianity like all others, must acknowledge that others experience that same uniqueness. Religions may and even should compare themselves to one another in public discourse, but no religion can claim an initial monopoly on the holy, the sacred, or the divine. Indeed, in any such monopolistic claim there lies embedded a genocidal impulse. One way I alone can be absolutely right is for all others to be dead. And one way for all others to be dead is for me, us, or our God to kill them. The challenge for the next millennium is to hold on to one's own faith with total integrity without having at the same time to negate or destroy that of others.

3

What Does John the Baptist
Have to Do with Jesus?

*I'm a religious [nun] for over forty years! . . . In this time of my
life, I find that the church has betrayed me! These wonderful
things the biblical scholars are discovering/recovering about Jesus
and the early church are things we should share and be revital-
ized by. I feel so alone and have no one to share the Eucharist
with. [It] seems meaningless unless we celebrate community. But
going to church on Sundays and other days just frustrates me. . . .
Is the bread we eat the Body of Christ or is it symbolic of his presence? . . . To be honest, it does not make too much difference to me.
What is happening is so important. Symbol can become a reality.*
A woman from Michigan

*My own experience leads me to believe that Crossan plays no
intentionally radical role, but rather has moved to the only place
his increasing archaeological, anthropological, sociological knowledge will allow him to dwell with integrity. . . . Mystery need not
be irrational. There is enough Mystery in the fact. . . that
Christianity still lingers though its leader was so swiftly dealt
with. And there is Mystery enough if Jesus' message of a radically egalitarian society, with no mediator necessary between anyone
and God, should tenaciously survive, long enough for archaeology,
anthropology, sociology and believers like Crossan to lift the veil
and beckon us to see the Light of that message still shining.*
A woman from Michigan

Thank you for your work with the Jesus Seminar and for your individual work on the life of Jesus. As I have been reading your books my faith has become deeper and more real. You and your colleagues have said things that I have always known deep in my heart. . . . Reading your work has helped me come to a deeper commitment in my faith, and to rededicate my life to teaching adults within the church. I had abandoned this Call ten years ago for personal and institutional reasons, but the model of faithful ministry that you present has given me the courage to re-evaluate that decision.

A woman from Michigan

I'm just a poor half-illiterate security guard who happens to believe that the Bible is the infallible Word of God. . . . My question to you, Dr. Crossan, is who appointed you as the heir to Jehoiakim? Who chose you to intellectually cut and burn the Gospel of God? Don't you see how you're hurting God's faithful?

A man from Alabama

I think you're on target. . . . If the work of the Jesus Seminar is not buried, and (so to speak) "Jesus speaks plainly once more"— then there are going to be some whollopping changes in this old world! There could be inflammatory response—like the Ayatollah's to Rushdie. There could be incredible malaise. . . you and the rest making about as much splash as a story in The National Inquirer—*or perhaps there might be a new reformation! Who knows.*

A man from South Carolina

Some time ago I listened to an interview with you on Station WBAY, The Idea Network of Wisconsin. . . . I was somewhat dismayed by your comments on Jesus and John the Baptist. (1) John did not put himself above Jesus; (2) John the Baptist said, "I must decrease, and you increase." (3) He is universally known as the forerunner *of Jesus. . . . I noticed the interviewer excellently raised questions against your diminishment of Jesus Christ.*

A woman from Wisconsin

For Jesus to have changed his view of John's mission and message at that time in the history of the Jews, in that place, would have confused his followers and destroyed his credibility. Only a Gentile, past or present could accept either the views of Christianity or your views. Few Jews, past or present could accept either position. Whatever you feel or believe about me, I believe you to be a courageous and worthwhile human being.

A man from Florida

Regarding the Baptizer—here in the Q Gospel—he seems to be a desert (hermitic) cynic-sage. Could it be that the Christians apocalyptacized him as they did Jesus? This does not undo Jesus' distinctiveness, but rather sees it in the difference between hermit and wayfarer.

A man from South Carolina

What about those details in Luke regarding the circumcision and presentation of Jesus in the Temple, about the prophecies of Anna and Simeon, and especially about that scene in the Temple when Jesus was twelve years old?

Recall what I mentioned earlier about Luke's parallel infancy stories in which Jesus is consistently exalted over John the Baptist. The stories mentioned in the question are part of that process. Jesus, of course, would have been circumcised, as were all male children of observant Jewish parents. But John the Baptist, for example, was presented to the world in the restricted space of his own home, whereas Jesus was presented to the world in the Temple itself. But it is especially that incident at twelve years of age that exalts Jesus far above John the Baptist, since the latter has no comparable story. That account of Jesus' precocious brilliance is very similar to what Josephus tells us about himself in his autobiography. When he was "a mere boy, about fourteen years old," he was so learned "that the chief priest and the leading men of the city used constantly to come to me for precise information on some particular in our ordinances" (*Life* 9). Those stories about Jesus or Josephus are standard assertions of moral and Biblical excellence. Neither of them offers factual details, but rather fictional ways of expressing a child's future importance by having it appear already in infancy or early adulthood.

It seems to me I remember an advertisement for a book about "the hidden years of Jesus." How much do we know about his childhood?

Really, nothing at all, in terms of history.

From time to time books are written that purport to tell long-lost stories of Jesus' childhood and youth. These are based on legends that never found their way into the New Testament. Pious imagination couldn't rest content with the restrained interlude of Luke, "And the child grew big and strong and full of wisdom, and God's favor was upon him." And so a fabric of legend was woven to wrap around the child Jesus. A second-century infancy gospel, for example, tells how when he was five years old Jesus took some soft clay and made twelve clay sparrows. A neighbor, who was offended because this broke the rule against working on the Sabbath, complained to Joseph, who rebuked his son. At this Jesus responded by clapping his hands and saying, "Off with you!" and the clay sparrows came to life and flew chirping away.

In such stories, the supernatural child was not always so cute and innocent in using his powers. We are told that when he got angry he cursed and withered those who got in his way, so that Joseph once commanded Mary, "Do not let him go outside the door, for all those who provoke him die." Not one of these legends, of course, has even a kernel of historical truth in it. The reality is that about Jesus' childhood and youth we know nothing. In itself that is not at all surprising. As so often happens in the early years of one famous only much later, nobody was watching or caring at that earlier period. Caesar Augustus, Roman emperor at the birth of Jesus, opened his official autobiography with the words "At the age of nineteen," thereby ignoring everything that had happened before that crucial adult moment.

When you talked about the birth stories, you mentioned that we know something about the social class into which Jesus was born. That must mean that we know something about his childhood.

That's true.

What we know about Jesus' social class comes from the same source that tells us about his brothers and sisters. In Mark 6:3 we read, "Is not this the *carpenter*, the son of Mary and brother of James, Joses, Judas, and Simon, and are not his sisters here with us?" That tells us not only that Jesus had four brothers, but what their names were, and that he had at least two sisters. It tells us more by identifying him as a carpenter. By the way, when Matthew tells the same story, he changes the question of the villagers to, "Is not this the carpenter's *son*?" So the tradition tells us that either Joseph or Jesus, or perhaps both (in a society where sons often followed in their fathers' footsteps), were carpenters. So the question is: what does that tell us about the social class into which Jesus was born?

It is important to avoid interpreting the word "carpenter" in modern terms. Nowadays a carpenter is a skilled, well-paid, respected member of the middle class. That wasn't true in the first century. The Greek word translated here as "carpenter" is "*tekton*." One scholar of the Greco-Roman world has published a "lexicon of snobbery" filled

with words used by literate upper class writers that show
their prejudice against illiterate lower class people. "*Tekton*"
is one of those words of disdain.

The Greco-Roman world was sharply divided between
those who had to work with their hands and those who did
not. On the upper class side of that chasm were four
groups: the *governing class*, who made up one to two percent
of the population but owned fifty percent of the land; the
priests, who might have owned as much as fifteen percent of
the land; the *retainers*, bureaucrats and army personnel who
served the governing and priestly classes; and the *merchants*,
who probably began in the lower classes but might have
ended up with substantial wealth and even political power.
On the lower class side of the chasm were, first, the *peasants*—the vast majority of the population, about two-thirds
of whose crop went to support the upper classes. They lived
at a bare subsistence level, and if drought or debt or disease
or death forced them off their land, they ended up as share-
croppers, tenant farmers, or worse. Next came the *artisans*,
about five percent of the population, who were lower than
the peasants in social class because they were usually
recruited from the ranks of dispossessed peasants. Finally,
beneath the artisans, came *degraded and expendable classes*—
who either had occupations that made them outcast, or
were reduced to begging, day labor, outlawry, or slavery.

If Jesus was from a carpenter family, he belonged to the
artisan class. That meant that he was lower than peasantry,
one of those pushed into the dangerous space between
peasants and the degradeds or expendables. He was, therefore, living on the edge of mere subsistence. And since at
the time of Jesus between ninety-five and ninety-seven percent of the Jewish state was illiterate, we must assume that
Jesus also was illiterate. Like most of his contemporaries in
an oral culture, he would have known the basic stories of
his tradition, but not the exact texts or arguments of the
learned scribes. That tells us, for example, that the scene in

Luke 4, where his adult skill in interpreting a passage in Isaiah astonishes his fellow villagers in Nazareth, is an invention of the gospel writer. What Luke does—as a literate skilled interpreter of scripture himself—is to rephrase the spoken challenge and charisma of Jesus in terms of scribal literacy and interpretation.

So, historically, we first meet Jesus as a man from lower class origins who goes with many others to be baptized by John in the Jordan River.

How sure are we that Jesus was baptized by John in the River Jordan?

Nothing is more certain about Jesus than this: that he was baptized by John in the Jordan River.

The reason for our certainty is that the Christian tradition shows increasing embarrassment about that baptism. Wherever we find the Church embarrassed by a tradition about Jesus, the odds are very strong that the tradition is rooted in actual history. And why was the Church embarrassed by the story of Jesus' baptism? Because it would seem to say that Jesus, like others, underwent baptism "for the forgiveness of sins," and because it seems to put John in a superior position as the one who baptized him.

So although Mark tells the baptism story without any defensive commentary, he immediately adds to it the story of a heavenly voice coming to Jesus saying, "You are my Son, the Beloved, with you I am well pleased." Matthew goes much further by having John protest to Jesus, "I need to be baptized by you, and do you come to me?" Finally, in the Gospel of John, John the Baptist witnesses to Jesus as the Son of God without any account of an actual baptism. By then the baptism of Jesus by John is gone and only the revelation about Jesus' significance remains. This whole process of development shows us that Christian communities were uneasy about suggesting that Jesus might have needed baptism for the forgiveness of sins or be in some way subordinate to John. Since the Church would hardly have invented a story that caused it such problems, that very embarrassment gives us confidence in the historical reality of the baptism.

When I think of John the Baptist, the first thing that comes to my mind is that gruesome story of a dancing girl asking for his head to be delivered to her on a platter. Why did John come to such an abrupt, violent end?

The biblical story that you refer to (found in Mark 6:17–29) tells how Herod Antipas sent men to arrest John because he had criticized Herod for marrying his brother Philip's wife. The irate woman in question then had her daughter, who danced before the king, reply to his offer to reward her by asking for John's head—a request which the king, having made a solemn vow, could not refuse. That is a marvelously dramatic story, but it is fiction. In fact, it's probably derived from an earlier and well-known Mediterranean horror story about a Roman senator in the preceding century who was expelled from office because he had a prisoner beheaded at a banquet to satisfy the curiosity of his mistress. In other words, it was a traditional story about how *not* to exercise power.

What, then, was the historical reason for the arrest and execution of John?

The first-century Jewish historian, Josephus, had this to say about the ministry of John the Baptist:

When others, too, joined the crowds about him, because they were aroused to the highest degree by his sermons, Herod became alarmed. Eloquence that had so great an effect on mankind might lead to some form of sedition, for it looked as if they would be guided by John in everything that they did. Herod decided, therefore, that it would be much better to strike first and be rid of him before his work led to an uprising, than to wait for an upheaval. . . . John, because of Herod's suspicions, was brought in chains to Machaerus . . . and there put to death.

Notice what we are told here: that John aroused people by his sermons, that many were willing to follow him in all that they did, and that the authorities feared that it might lead to some form of sedition, or even to an uprising. Obviously, John was seen as posing a threat much more serious than merely commenting on the marital arrangements of Herod Antipas.

Take a look at what the *Q Gospel* says about the content of those sermons of John that so aroused people (Matthew 3:7–12):

You offspring of vipers! Who warned you to flee from the coming fury? Change your ways if you have changed your mind. Don't say, "We have Abraham as our father." I am telling you, God can raise up children for Abraham from these stones. Even now the ax is aimed at the root of the trees. Every tree that does not bear good fruit is cut down and thrown into the fire. . . . I am plunging you in water; but one who is stronger than I is coming, one whose sandals I am not worthy to touch. He will overwhelm you with holy spirit and fire. His winnowing fork is in his hand to clear his threshing floor and gather the wheat into his granary. The chaff he will burn with a fire that no one can put out.

What does this mean? John was talking about a God who was going to come very soon as an avenger. God is like a forester with an ax separating good trees from bad ones, like a thresher separating grain from chaff. In John's fiery vision there are just two ways, the good and the bad, and the time is short for people to decide for one side or the other. Like ancient prophets he announces that God is coming to set right an evil situation and to save an oppressed people. John is, in other words, an apocalyptic preacher announcing the coming of an avenging God.

An "apocalyptic preacher"? What does "apocalyptic" mean?

"Apocalyptic" is a word that takes us to the very heart of my argument about John—and indeed Jesus. So we need to take some time to get clear about it. But first, let me sketch in a bit of historical background.

Down to the present day we often talk about the *Pax Romana*—the Roman Peace. We have, in other words, accepted Rome's self-understanding as expressed in the famous lines of Virgil's *Aeneid*:

> *Roman, remember by your strength to rule*
> *Earth's peoples—for your arts are to be these:*
> *To pacify, to impose the rule of law,*
> *To spare the conquered, battle down the proud.*

That is a very benign view of Roman power and rule. But think for a moment what that rule looked like and felt like from below—from the viewpoint of the conquered ones.

The Roman historian Tacitus wrote a biography of his father-in-law, Agricola, who governed Britain in the late first century. In that biography he has a rebel general describe the Roman Empire from his point of view: "To plunder, butcher, steal, these things they misname empire: they make a desolation and they call it peace."

That is the view of the *Pax Romana* from the underside.

And so the question becomes: how do oppressed people react when they have been conquered militarily, overwhelmed economically, beaten down socially? There are two ways. One way is to fight again and again, usually losing against overwhelming power. In the first century there were a number of such Jewish uprisings against Roman power—often sparked by *messianic leaders*, so called because they were thought to be "anointed" by God to restore the kingdom promised to David and his successors. Often these messianic leaders expected supernatural assistance—in the style of their remembered traditions. A second response is that of *apocalyptic prophets*. These do not look for a military rebellion by human beings, but announce that God's own power is soon going to accomplish what human resistance cannot accomplish, namely, a total victory of good over evil and the arrival of a world of justice and goodness.

The latter is what I mean by "apocalypticism." It is waiting for God's action to end intolerable oppression and evil and bring a new, just, and perfect world into being. And what I am arguing is that John the Baptist was the first in a series of apocalyptic prophets who appeared in the Jewish homeland until it was destroyed in the late 60s for rebellion against Rome.

So there were others preaching in the style of John the Baptist?

From both Josephus and the New Testament we know that there were a number of leaders who took throngs of people out into the desert, promising to show them signs of God's forthcoming deliverance. And here it's very important to see the significance of going out into the desert and recrossing the Jordan. Remember that Moses and Joshua in ancient times led the Israelites through a time of desert wandering and into the Promised Land. What these apocalyptic prophets were doing was taking people back into the wilderness, crossing the Jordan, and reentering the Promised Land as their ancestors had done with God's assistance. We're even told that one such prophet announced that at his command the walls of Jerusalem would fall down. That reminds us of Joshua marching around the walls of Jericho waiting for a spectacular victory from God. The apocalyptic prophets thus hoped to do by divine power what they could not do by mere human strength.

That is why John gathered people for baptism at the Jordan River.

But John never led people in a mass movement against the regime, did he? All he did was baptize individuals.

True. John was *like* the other apocalyptic prophets in that he announced and awaited God's intervention to set right the oppressions and evils of the present day. But John was *unlike* many other apocalyptic prophets in that he did not gather followers together to lead them *en masse* into the Promised Land. John's strategy seems to have been different. When people came to him, he kept sending them back from the wilderness, through the Jordan, purified and forgiven into the Promised Land, there to await the imminent coming of the avenging, saving God. In essence, John was forming a giant system of purified individuals—a network of ticking time bombs all over the Jewish homeland. Because of John, when Jesus began his ministry, he found already a vast network of people expectant, eager, waiting for God's power to be revealed.

So Jesus began as a disciple of John?

Jesus was certainly baptized by John in the Jordan River. Like many others, Jesus was part of a ritual reenacting of the Moses and Joshua stories of the conquest of the Promised Land by God's power. So Jesus became part of that network within the Jewish homeland of people waiting for God's coming. What were they waiting for? Presumably for God to do what they lacked power to do—destroy Roman power. Jesus began as an apocalyptic believer. He began in the tradition of John.

We have ample evidence in gospel stories of Jesus' high opinion of John. In the *Q Gospel* (Matthew 11:7–9 or Luke 7:24–26) Jesus speaks of John as not only a prophet but "much more than a prophet." He also says (Matthew 11:11 or Luke 7:28) that "no one born of a woman is greater than John; yet the least in God's kingdom is greater than he." In those last words we are introduced to a *separation* between Jesus and John. Jesus has regarded John as not only a prophetic figure, but as greater than the prophets. Yet at the same time he now announces that the least in the Kingdom of God is greater than John. What does this mean?

I want to return later to that phrase the "Kingdom of God," but for now I'll simply say that Jesus makes a distinction between John as the culmination of the past and the newly arrived Kingdom of God which holds the future. Something new is happening, Jesus is saying. It belongs not to John in the desert, but to the child in the Kingdom. What this means is that *Jesus has changed his view* about John's mission and message. For Jesus it is no longer enough simply to await God's intervention to bring in a new world. One must enter a new world—which he calls the Kingdom—*here and now*. The Kingdom is an ever-present reality in which Jesus lived and into which he invited all whom he met to enter. Perhaps it was John's execution that led Jesus to understand that God did not and would not change the world through imminent apocalyptic restoration. Jesus would begin to move in a new direction: It is not that we are waiting for God, but that God is waiting for us.

But Jesus does seem to be an apocalyptic figure—at least as the gospel writers portray him. What are we to make of sayings like "The Son of Man will come on the clouds of heaven"?

The question about the "Son of Man" sayings has been one of the most hotly debated in New Testament studies. My conclusion is simply this: That while New Testament writers attribute the title "Son of Man" to Jesus—clearly meaning an apocalyptic deliverer who is to come—Jesus did not refer to himself by such a title. Jesus used "son of man" in a generic sense, simply to mean (and this was the original meaning of the phrase) *human being*. But apocalyptic use of the phrase "Son of Man" with respect to Jesus was a tradition that grew up about Jesus after his death.

There are many different ways in which a radical challenge can be thrown down to present worldly powers. *Ascetics* withdraw from the world into caves, deserts, or monasteries. *Nihilists* try to destroy the world with words, deeds, or bombs. *Apocalyptic prophets* announce that the world is so evil and beyond human remedy that only immediate divine intervention can set it straight. *Jesus comes with a different strategy*. He challenges the present structures of life through the creation of a new kind of community which here and now embodies the values of "God's Kingdom."

The difference between John and Jesus is made crystal clear in a segment of the *Q Gospel* (Matthew 11:18–19 or Luke 7:33–34):

> *John did not come eating and drinking, and they are saying, "He is demon possessed." The son of man [that is, Jesus] has come eating and drinking, and they say, "Look at him, a glutton and a drunkard, a friend of tax collectors and sinners."*

The contrast is between a *fasting* John and a *feasting* Jesus. John lives an ascetic life, alone, out in the desert.

Jesus gathers people around a dinner table, building a new kind of human community. In chapters to come I will say more about what that means. What we have established so far is what John was, how Jesus began, and how eventually, in his own words and in the eyes of others, Jesus became something very different from John—indeed, almost the exact opposite of the Baptist. Jesus certainly challenges the world in which he lives, but in a very different way from the apocalyptic prophet who announces the imminent judgment of God.

I have read that John the Baptist lived for a time at Qumran among the Essenes. Is that accurate?

Most people have heard by now of the Dead Sea Scrolls. These are manuscripts, some complete, but the vast majority in fragments, discovered in caves along the northwestern shore of the Dead Sea in the Jewish homeland. It is generally held that the Essenes, dissident priests who had broken with the official Temple priesthood about a century and a half before the time of Jesus, lived in the enclave now called Qumran and buried their library in the caves before the attack of the Romans in the first Jewish revolt of 66–74. Those Essenes had withdrawn into the desert, but west of the Jordan, unlike John to the east; and they awaited the arrival of twin Messiahs, one priestly and one lay, unlike John who awaited the arrival of God without any mention of a preceding Messiah (before, of course, the Christian gospels had adopted John the Baptist as the forerunner of Jesus). John's once-and-for-all baptism, by crossing from the desert through the Jordan River into the Promised Land, is totally different from the daily purification rituals at Qumran. I see John's movement, therefore, as quite distinct from that of Qumran, oriented toward the general populace rather than an educated group living in isolated community.

4

What Did Jesus Teach?

Congratulations on compromising and denigrating the beautiful thing we call "faith" and reducing it to your empirical and media-centered "scientific" search for the TRUTH! . . . I am not some religious extremist and do not belong to a televised "group" or anything. I am simply a father and husband struggling to make my own contribution in this life and support a higher sense of morality and values within my family life. . . . Please review what you are doing and I pray that you stop this harmful process and affront to the very One that gave us His Son for our salvation.

A man from Texas

Rarely if ever have we read anything quite so revolutionary, quite so liberating and so deeply challenging as your book. I have long since stopped thinking of Jesus as God (i.e. the Trinitarian ontology) although the metaphor of God-dying-in-Jesus allows some very challenging images. But I clung to an ontology of resurrection (a la Paul). Your book has shown me that even that is not necessary to be a follower of Jesus and confess Jesus as Lord.

A couple from South Africa

Prof. Crossan seems to suffer from selective reading of the Bible. . . . Jesus clearly champions the poor, sick and oppressed. He clearly tries to change the hearts of people to care and share for them. . . . Crossan ignores the portrayal that Jesus has rich friends without telling them to give all they have to the poor as he did the rich young lawyer. The obvious lesson is that Jesus felt that differences in living standards were acceptable providing that one is responsible in one's use of one's talents and resources by substantially aiding the poor and oppressed. Communal living did not last very long even amongst those committed early Christians.

A man from California

[In] thirty years of pastoral work, it just has not been possible to keep up with the intense debate which has obviously framed so much of your own work. During my time [at seminary] pastoral concerns were at the top of the list. I found that epilogue [to Who Killed Jesus?*] to be one of the most refreshing perspectives on faith and scholarship and commitment I have read in a very long time. This letter is intended to simply thank you for strongly presented scholarship. I may or may not agree with your conclusions; it will take some time to decipher much of what I find. But I am very grateful that you took time in this particular debate to be personal and encouraging to others who work as pastors.*

A man from Texas

Professor Crossan, I say this in Christian love *and care for your life* in eternity, *that you reconsider just* who Jesus really is *and that* HE *lives even right now at the Right Hand of God the Father, interceding for you and all who* have believed in Him— *as Saviour and Lord—Coming Bridegroom and King of Kings and Lord of Lords—May the Lord help you to see, in Christ's love,*

A man from Alabama

Where I'm coming from right now is to accept the historical findings—and begin to reflect on these sayings, individually and in small groups and try to perform them in our lives.

A man from Arizona

I was very unhappy with your position on a revised mission for Jesus and your concept of the Son of Man, Kingdom of God and how to achieve it. I felt that things I had come to believe about Jesus were being attacked and decided to defend, I have never done this before. . . . It is reasonable for me to think that Jesus believed in the imminent ending of the world and in his return in splendor before this generation passed away. I believe that Jesus was like John. They both preached for people to repent and that the Kingdom of God was at hand.

A man from Florida

I am now re-reading the book [Jesus: A Revolutionary Biography] in order to answer a few questions I have. . . . Could you define the God you said is "available to you (and all of us)"? My second question would be . . . define the Kingdom of God. My feeling is that it is here and now at the table described in the parable where we all sit down and eat together without any class, religious, ethnic or economic lines or distinctions among us.

A man from New Hampshire

You usually hear that Jesus taught about the Kingdom of God. Is that right and what does it mean?

We have an immediate problem with that phrase "Kingdom of God." Matthew, for example, prefers to avoid the name of God out of reverence for its holiness, so he usually rephrases that expression as the "Kingdom of Heaven." We tend to hear that as the "Kingdom *in* Heaven," as if Jesus was talking not about earth, but about heaven; not about this life, but about the next life. Nothing could be farther from the truth. And to understand Jesus' meaning we must not separate religion and politics, ethics and economics in that first-century world. "Kingdom of God" means what this world would look like if God, not Caesar, sat on its imperial throne; if God, not Caesar, was openly, clearly, and completely in charge. It is, at the same time, an absolutely religious and absolutely political concept. It is absolutely moral and absolutely economic at the same time. How would God run the world? How does God want this world run? It is not about heaven, but about earth.

As we have already seen, for one group of people in the Jewish homeland—apocalypticists, like John the Baptist—the Kingdom of God was understood as a *future* reality. Not only was it future, but it depended on the *overpowering intervention of God* in human affairs to bring justice and peace to an earth felt to be almost hopelessly mired in injustice and oppression. At the very most, the faithful could prepare for or assist the arrival of the Kingdom, but its accomplishment would come by God's power alone. And although apocalyptists were serenely vague about the details of that coming Kingdom, they were clear that it would be objective and visible to all—but with appropriately different fates for the good and bad.

There was, however, another way of thinking about the Kingdom of God. Instead of us waiting for God to begin an apocalyptic intervention, God is waiting for us to begin a social revolution. It is, in both uses, the Kingdom *of God*, because neither solution is deemed possible by simple human endeavor. But a divine apocalyptic intervention is very different from a divine social revolution; and Jesus, having abandoned John the Baptist's hope for the former, turned instead to announce the latter.

Why continue to use an expression like "Kingdom of God"? Why not replace it with, say, the "Community of God"? That is surely more appropriate than anything with an exclusively male word like "king" in it.

For several reasons that word "kingdom" poses some problems as the translation of the New Testament Greek word "*basileia*." For one thing, the "king-" part of the word is chauvinistic. For another, the "-dom" part of the word makes it sound as though we're talking about some locality, some piece of geography. And a third problem is that in our contemporary world we have no real sense of what it meant to be ruled by monarchs. To be sure, we watch with fascination the pomp and ceremony that surround the few remaining crowned heads in the world—like Queen Elizabeth II of England—yet we all recognize that her role is traditional and ceremonial, but not powerful.

In the Mediterranean world into which Jesus was born, however, the king had power indeed. And it was not only Jewish apocalyptic prophets who were concerned about *basileia*—kingly rule—in the first century. *Basileia* was a common subject in the Hellenistic world, and the issue was this: how should power be exercised in a just and humane way? The gospels are wrestling with the contrast between how *human* power and *divine* power are exercised. When Jesus uses a phrase like the "Kingdom of God," he is talking about *what the world would look like if God were directly and immediately in charge*. What would the world be like if God sat on Caesar's throne? The Kingdom of God is a symbol for an ideal description of human life, transcending and calling into question all existing forms of human rule and social order. A term other than "kingdom" might lack that political-religious challenge.

Members of the Jesus Seminar proposed translating the Greek word as "God's imperial rule" to emphasize the contrast with Caesar's imperial rule. It is that critical social edge and subversive political tone that I try to maintain by holding on to "kingdom" rather than "community." Were I to use that latter term, I would lose Jesus' political-religious challenge: whose is the kingdom, the power, and the glory? God's or Caesar's? But, by all means, use "community" instead of "kingdom" as long as the subversive social challenge and critical political edge are present in the meaning.

An example might help. Imagine a German Christian

community in the early 1930s that called Jesus "*der Führer*" and insisted that there was only one such *Führer*. In itself that is a very ordinary German word meaning "leader"; yet, after Hitler's advent, that Christian usage clearly would have meant: Jesus is our leader, Hitler is not.

Use, therefore, any modern translation you want for "Kingdom of God," but remember that it should always have overtones of high treason. Similarly, to say that Jesus was Lord meant that Caesar was not. Translate "Lord" with any contemporary expression you deem appropriate, as long as it is one that could get you killed.

Are you saying that the Kingdom movement was just promoting a worldly, political realm?

No. Let me introduce a very important scholarly adjective: "eschatological." It comes from a Greek word meaning "about the end of this world," and it can be applied properly to either divine apocalyptic intervention or divine social revolution. Recall that situation just discussed, when one believes the world has become seriously and profoundly evil and therefore needs serious redemption. Such profound redemption might be termed "radical," "ideal," "utopian," "counter-cultural," or "eschatological." All those words indicate an ending of this present normal world and its replacement by a perfect alternative. A divine apocalyptic intervention or a divine social revolution are two alternative scenarios for such an ideal, utopian, or eschatological solution. The former is the message of John's Baptism movement. The latter is the message of Jesus' Kingdom movement.

When Jesus was teaching did his followers record his words about the Kingdom of God as they were spoken?

Jesus, we must always remember, was not a literate, upper class scribe, but an illiterate peasant. He spoke with an oral brilliance that few academically trained persons ever attain. Whenever we read words ascribed to him that were written down by literate classes decades and even generations after his death, we must recognize that his first audiences would have retained only the most striking images, the most startling analogies, the most forceful plot summaries of stories that might have taken hours or more to tell.

I want to turn now to some practical consequences that Jesus draws from his teaching concerning the Kingdom of God. Why does he attack so fiercely what we might term "family values"?

In twentieth-century America the supreme value is probably *individualism*, but the supreme value of the first century might rather be called "*groupism*." That value was based on kinship and gender relationships. What we find in Jesus are some biting sayings about Mediterranean family values. Here are three examples.

The first example is from Mark 3:31–35:

Then his mother and his brothers came; and standing outside, they sent to him and called him. . . . And he replied, "Who are my mother and my brothers?" And looking at those who sat around him, he said, "Here are my mother and my brothers! Whoever does the will of God is my brother and sister and mother."

Jesus makes an almost savage attack on family values as they were understood in the Mediterranean world—and makes it more than once. Then, as now, the family was a group to which one was *assigned*. But in the text just quoted,

Jesus downplays the family in favor of another kind of group that is *open to all who wish to join it*. For Jesus, the given family unit, the kinship unit, is no longer primary. What is primary is a new community of persons who become "family" to one another in their common effort to do the will of God in the world.

A second example is that of a woman in the crowd around Jesus who blurted out a blessing upon his mother: "How fortunate is the womb that bore you, and the breasts that you sucked!" (Luke 11:27). But in response Jesus turned back the compliment, saying, "How fortunate, rather, are those who listen to God's teaching and observe it!" The woman declares that Mary is blessed because of Jesus. In typical Mediterranean fashion, she believes that a woman's greatness derives from being the mother of a famous son. Though it's a common attitude in a patriarchal society, Jesus will have none of it. What he offers is a blessedness that is open to anyone who wants it, without distinction of sex or gender, infertility or maternity.

A final example is from the *Q Gospel*, in Luke 12:51–53:

> *"Do you think that I have come to bring peace to the earth? No, I tell you, but rather division! From now on five in one household will be divided, three against two and two against three; they will be divided: father against son and son against father, mother against daughter and daughter against mother, mother-in-law against her daughter-in-law and daughter-in-law against mother-in-law."*

The usual interpretation of this passage is that families will become divided as some believe in Jesus and others refuse to put their faith in him. But I think the point has nothing to do with family *faith*, but with family *power*. Notice that the dividing line in the parable is between the generations. Jesus pictures a typical Mediterranean family with five members, mother and father, unmarried daughter, married son and his wife, all living under one roof. Jesus says he will tear it apart. His attack is on the Mediterranean family's power arrangement, which has father and mother in authority over son, daughter, and daughter-in-law.

This story, in fact, helps us to understand all of Jesus' stories and teachings about family life. The family is society in miniature, the setting in which we learn patterns of love, hate, helping, abusing. Not all families are Norman Rockwell scenes of warmth and nurturing. Since family life involves power, it also invites the abuse of power, and that is the point of Jesus' critique. His ideal group is contrary to customary human social arrangements, a group that is open and equally accessible to all under God. In the Kingdom of God there is no abuse of power. All are welcome, all are equal, and all are alike under the will and purpose of God.

Even in our twentieth-century democratic society, far removed from the authority patterns of Jesus' world, we have become painfully aware of abuses of power in family life. The phrase "domestic violence" is heard much more than it was a generation ago. We now know that gross abuses of power often lurk behind the facade of domestic tranquillity. So whether in the first century or the twentieth, Jesus' critique has something to say: No given structure of family life is absolute; all structures exist for human nurturing. Family life, like all human life, comes under the critique of the Kingdom of God. Family life, like other forms of human association, exists for purposes of justice and love.

The sayings of Jesus about society seem just as radical or even as negative as those about the family. Why is that?

I use just one example here, but it is a very radical saying of Jesus that takes us deeper into his sense of the Kingdom. This saying is found in four different versions. Luke's version is: "Blessed are you who are poor, for yours is the kingdom of God" (Luke 6:20). What we see in the other versions is how uncomfortable the tradition became with that saying in its stark form and how hard interpreters worked to soften it.

For example, when Matthew records the phrase, it becomes: "Blessed are *the poor in spirit*, for theirs is the Kingdom of heaven" (Matthew 5:3). Matthew changes "poor" to refer not to the economically destitute but to the religiously humble, thus blunting the force of Jesus' word. Moreover, in the letter of James, the poor are called "rich in faith and heirs of the kingdom which he has promised" (James 2:5). The Kingdom is now no longer a present reality, but a promised future, and the poor are those who are *rich in faith*. Both Matthew and James have filed away the rough edges of a saying linking the poverty-stricken and the Kingdom.

Moreover, we have a very serious problem when the Greek word in the gospel text is translated as "poor." That word really means "destitute." The Greek language has a separate word for "poor," which describes a peasant family that makes a bare subsistence living from year to year. But the actual Greek word used in the beatitude refers to a family that has been pushed by disease or debt or drought or death off the land and into destitution and begging. The *poor* person has to work hard but has enough to survive, while the *destitute* person has nothing at all. In other words, Jesus did not simply declare the poor blessed—a class that for all practical purposes included the entire peasantry— but declared the destitute and the beggars blessed.

Well, what on earth does that mean? Did Jesus really think that beggars were specially blessed by God—as if all the destitute were nice people and all the upper class were evil?

I don't think this saying reflects a naive or romantic illusion about how charming it is to be destitute. I do think that it is important to hear this, not just in an individual sense, but in a social sense. That is, Jesus and his fellow peasants found themselves in a structured system of injustice. In situations of oppression, especially where injustice is so built in to the system that it seems normal or even necessary, the only ones who are innocent or blessed are those who have been squeezed out deliberately as human junk from the operations of the system. If Jesus were to speak this message among us today, it might come out like this: "Only the homeless are innocent." And that is, of course, a terrifying saying. It is terrifying because, like his words against the family, it focuses not just on individual abuse of power but on abuse in its systemic forms. Such sayings cut because while we may feel innocent of *personal* wrongdoing, as participants in *social systems* that are unjust, none of us has clean hands or a clear conscience.

The most important conclusion from that saying is that the Kingdom of God is a critique of systemic rather than just individual evil. It not only says, as it were, do not rape or brutalize your slave, but claims that slavery is against the radical justice or absolute equality demanded by God. Jesus' criticism is systemic and structural rather than individual and personal.

So far we have been speaking of the sayings or aphorisms of Jesus, but what about his stories or parables? Is not Jesus, above all, a teller of tales, a speaker of parables?

If you read any of Jesus' parables today it takes you less than a minute to do so in most cases. But those versions are only plot summaries. An actual telling or, better, acting of a parable might have taken Jesus an hour or so and must have involved frequent audience interaction to agree or disagree, comment on or discuss. In such a situation, Jesus' parables would have been scenes of debate not just about religion or theology but about politics and economics. They would have steadily raised audience consciousness about the systemic injustice of imperial rule and colonialism. They would have drawn regular attention to the divergent fates of aristocrats and peasants and to that terrible line between poverty and destitution. When you read a parable, think of the divergent responses, probably loud and immediate, from different classes or genders within a common audience. A parable empowers rather than dominates an audience. It challenges them to think and judge for themselves. It is the most appropriate teaching technique for a Kingdom of God in which God empowers rather than dominates, challenges rather than controls.

But what would that have to do with, say, the parable of the mustard seed which simply says that the Kingdom starts out very small but ends up great and large?

That's a common interpretation. But we need to take a look at Mediterranean mustard plants—and also at nesting birds. It's true that mustard plants do start as proverbially small seeds and grow into shrubs that are three or four feet high, or even higher. But I really don't think that we have yet got to the real point of Jesus' parable.

Pliny the Elder, who died in the year 79 when he approached too close to the erupting Mount Vesuvius, wrote about the mustard plant in his book *Natural History*. He described its pungent taste and "fiery effect"—which he thought was very beneficial to the health. He noted that the plant grows entirely wild, although it can be improved when transplanted, and added, "When it has once been sown, it is scarcely possible to get the place free of it, as the seed when it falls germinates at once." In other words, he is

saying that the mustard plant tends to take over where it is
not wanted, that it tends to get out of control, and that it is
difficult to eradicate. Jesus claimed that this new Kingdom
of God is like a pungent shrub with dangerous takeover
properties. In fact, in cultivated areas it tends to attract
birds where they are not wanted—no farmer likes to have
them around eating up his seeds and grains. Again, this is a
startling metaphor: the Kingdom is a pest to those who
own carefully cultivated gardens. Do you think landowners,
tenant farmers, day laborers, unemployed workers, or destitute beggars would all respond alike to that startling
image of the Kingdom of God as a mustard plant?

***So parables were more than just "sermon illustrations"?
They forced people to make decisions about their meaning?***

Take a look at a parable of Jesus which helps answer that
question affirmatively. In fact, it helps us understand all
those other sayings about the Kingdom of God to which we
have so far referred. It is found in several different versions;
I am quoting from the *Gospel of Thomas 64*.

*Jesus said, "A person was receiving guests. When he had
prepared the dinner, he sent his servant to invite the guests.
The servant went to the first and said to that one, 'My
master invites you.' That person said, 'Some merchants owe
me money; they are coming to me tonight. I must go and
give them instructions. Please excuse me from dinner.' The
servant went to another and said to that one, 'My master
has invited you.' That person said to the servant, 'I have
bought a house and I have been called away for a day. I shall
have no time.' The servant went to another and said to that
one, 'My master invites you.' That person said to the servant, 'My friend is to be married and I am to arrange the*

banquet. I shall not be able to come. Please excuse me from dinner.' The servant went to another and said to that one, 'My master invites you.' That person said to the servant, 'I have bought an estate and I am going to collect the rent. I shall not be able to come. Please excuse me.' The servant returned and said to his master, 'The people whom you invited to dinner have asked to be excused.' The master said to his servant, 'Go out on the streets and bring back whomever you find to have dinner.' Buyers and merchants [will] not enter the places of my father."

The final sentence, "Buyers and merchants will not enter the places of my father," is Thomas's interpretation of the parable's meaning. When Luke tells the story, he mentions "outcasts" who are called into the meal, and Matthew mentions "good and bad" who are gathered. But behind all those separate interpretations we can see a common story line.

Jesus tells a story about a person who prepares a dinner party and sends out his servant to invite friends to attend. Each one of the persons invited has an excuse for being unable to come. So here is a dinner ready, but a room empty. And so the host sends his servant to replace the absent guests with anyone he can find off the streets.

Think about that situation for a minute. If anyone had been brought in off the street, there undoubtedly would have been sexes, classes, ranks all mixed up together. Anyone could have been reclining next to anyone else: female next to male, free next to slave, socially high next to socially low, ritually pure next to ritually impure. And that, of course, would have been a social nightmare and a threat to all the carefully constructed conventions of social life in the first century.

Well, not only in the first century. Can you seriously imagine someone in the present day throwing a dinner party and just inviting anybody who happened to be wandering down the street?

Exactly the point. Think for a moment of a beggar coming to your door. Maybe you would give that beggar some food to take with him on the road. But would you invite him into your kitchen for a meal, or bring him into the dining room to have supper with your family, or have him come back Saturday night for a supper with a group of your friends? Or again, suppose you were the CEO in a large company. Think of the difference between holding a cocktail party in the office for all employees, a lunch at the restaurant for middle managers, or a private dinner party for your vice-presidents at home. In the twentieth century, as in the first century, who we invite to eat with us in what sort of situation says a great deal about social standing and relationships.

So eating is not simply a physiological act to get rid of hunger pangs. Anthropologists tell us that *the "rules" of eating are miniature models of a society's rules about people's relationships and behavior*. What we do at the dinner table serves as a map of economic, social, and political differences.

To take a twentieth-century example, think back to the United States at the start of the civil rights movement. Think of the furor that erupted at a Woolworth lunch counter when black young people sat there to order a sandwich or a Coke. This modern, enlightened, democratic society had rules about who could eat and drink where, when, and with whom. It was literally against the law for blacks to eat in certain places, and certainly for blacks and whites to eat together. That segregated lunch counter was a miniature model of the patterns of association in the segregated society as a whole. So when young people, black and white, broke the rules and sat around tables together to eat (or rode in the same bus), they were creating a new model of what the society should look like. The *segregated table* symbolized human separation and discrimination; the *open table* symbolized human community, oneness, equality. And that is exactly what was going on in the ministry of Jesus.

But a parable is just a story, isn't it? Who would ever take it literally?

It was only a story, of course, but it was a very pointed story that challenged the society's miniature model, the table, as a place of hierarchy and separation. And it was really more than a parable because *Jesus lived out his parable* by calling around his table people of different genders, social classes, and religious scruples. Do you remember that accusation mentioned earlier that John the Baptist was possessed because he fasted, and that Jesus was a glutton and drunkard because he ate with sinners, tax collectors, and even whores. That, of course, is but nasty name-calling in both cases, but even name-calling must have a logic, must have some basis in fact to be valuable as invective. Jesus' *living out* that parable of the open table is what produced the accusation that he was a glutton and drunkard, a friend of tax collectors and sinners. The critics were saying, in other words, that he made no appropriate distinctions and discriminations. And since *women* were present when he was at table, especially unmarried women, the obvious accusation would be that "Jesus eats with whores"—"whore" being the standard insult directed at any female who was outside socially approved male control. So all of those terms—tax collectors, sinners, whores—are derogatory terms for those with whom, in the opinion of the name-callers, open and free association should be avoided.

So for Jesus, the Kingdom of God is pictured as a new

kind of meal arrangement. A nondiscriminating table depicts in miniature a nondiscriminating society, and this vision clashed fundamentally with the basic values of ancient Mediterranean culture. It is not too soon to suggest that one can see, in the outrage that followed Jesus' new habits of table association, the reason for the arrest and execution that would later bring his ministry to its end.

Where does the Last Supper fit into this picture?

Our sense of that meal has been colored, of course, by the ritual traditions of our churches, whether called "Communion," "the Lord's Supper," or "the Eucharist." Jesus may well have had a last meal with his disciples, but the historical question is whether he instituted a new Passover meal, symbolizing his martyrdom, with the instruction to repeat it in his memory. The evidence is mixed. Paul certainly knows about such an institution (l Corinthians 11:23–25). But the *Didache*, a late-first-century document, describes a communal eating custom among Christians and shows no awareness of a ritual deriving from the Last Supper, no connection with the Passover meal, and no commemoration of the death of Jesus. So I would put the situation this way: What Jesus left behind was the tradition of open eating as a sign of the inclusiveness and equality of life in the Kingdom of God. Later, certain Christian groups created the Last Supper ritual, adding a commemoration of Jesus' death to that tradition of shared meals.

You referred earlier to the civil rights movement in the U.S. as an illustration of Jesus' movement in the first century. Isn't there a problem here that when you speak about the openness and equality between people that Jesus was modeling, you are painting a picture with contemporary colors? Aren't you just projecting modern democratic values backward into the first century?

No, I am picturing something much more radical than our experience of contemporary democracy.

Let me put it this way. Those who, like peasants, live with the boot on their neck have a choice between two different dreams. One dream is of a world in which they in turn can put their boots on those other necks. That is the quite understandable hope or even plan of *revenge*. But an alternative dream is of *justice*—a world in which there would never again be any boots on any necks. Consider, for example, these words of an unnamed peasant woman from Sicily, speaking to a northern Italian journalist during a peasant uprising in 1893:

> *We want everybody to work, as we work. There should no longer be either rich or poor. All should have bread for themselves and for their children. We should all be equal. I have five small children and only one little room, where we have to eat and sleep and do everything, while so many lords have ten or twelve rooms, entire palaces. . . . It will be enough to put all in common and to share with justice what is produced.*

There were in the first century plenty of people in the Jewish homeland who looked toward a future of revenge. Jesus was among the ones who envisioned instead a future of justice. The open table, the end of abusive power, the radical equality that is expressed in Jesus' sayings, and modelings of the Kingdom of God are not simply a prefiguring of modern democracy. They are more radical, more terrifying than anything that we have ever imagined. And even if we can never fulfill, or even accept that vision, we should not try to explain it away as something less. We should avoid doing what even the gospel writers frequently did, namely, taming the words and deeds of Jesus to make them easier to understand and to do. The vision of the Kingdom of God that Jesus offered may not be immediately translatable into every real human social situation. Its relevance is that, as vision, it always exists in creative tension with every social situation and all customary human arrangements—hopefully, spurring us to greater efforts to remove abuses and to embody justice. It announces a God of radical justice who calls us to establish nothing less than that on earth. If we reply that such is not possible, God might respond that, in the long run then, neither is the world.

Was Jesus' message about the Kingdom of God all talk or did it involve acton as well? Did Jesus offer an idea or a program?

We have already seen that Jesus lived in a time of social turmoil, and that a phrase like the "Kingdom of God" had social and political meanings for those who heard it. It was, one could say, one hundred percent religious but also one hundred percent political, one hundred percent theological but one hundred percent social and economic as well. Is it possible that Jesus' teaching was merely *spiritual* and not related to the crisis his people were facing? Why, in any event, would oppressed peasants listen to him? It is a particular temptation for those of us who are scholars or preachers to interpret Jesus in purely intellectual terms as a part of the history of ideas. But what I want to insist upon here is that Jesus not only *discussed* the Kingdom of God, but *acted it out* and invited others to act it out as well. If, in fact, all he had done was talk about the Kingdom, lower Galilee would probably have greeted him with a great big peasant yawn.

I have argued that it was Jesus' active practice of inviting people to a common table in violation of the customary social norms that brought about those nasty accusations that he was "a glutton and drunkard, a friend of tax collectors and sinners." His open table was intended as a miniature model for society. I want to insist that the same thing was happening with the *healings* of Jesus. They are not simply individual acts of compassion, but are another way of modeling the Kingdom of God in opposition to the established patterns of society's life. If we are not to reduce Jesus to a teacher of abstract ideas alone, it is crucially important for us to understand his free healing as well as his open table. And that points us into the next chapter.

5

Did Jesus Perform Miracles?

[In Haiti] I have seen a little girl try to ease her hunger by eating dirt. When I approached her, she covered her lips to conceal the mouthful of grit and pebbles, but tiny telltale stones glistened on her lips and chin. . . . I feel so stirred and inspired by Crossan's description of Jesus as a radical egalitarian who broke down barriers to celebrate table fellowship with all manner of people. I just wish we could set a table for the little Haitian boy who cried in my arms last night. . . . I asked him why he looked so sad. He burst into tears, eyes full of pain, and whispered, "I'm hungry."
An American woman in Haiti

I have just finished reading your book and thank you for writing it. After a while I will have to read it again to understand much of it. It is very interesting but does not go into many things that bother me. All my life I have had difficulty with the concept of God, and have been working on it. What did Jesus say about God?

A woman from Puerto Rico

Thanks to your books, I am now in the process of "un-doing" thirty years of "doing theology and calling it history and doing Christian apologetics and calling it academic scholarship." If I were only fifty years younger, you would find my name on your class lists. . . . Thanks a million for making my old age more exciting.

A man from Florida

There are still secrets and mysteries to be revealed. But the Bible says there is nothing hidden that will not be revealed. I doubt that it would be revealed to a professor of religion at DePaul University. Most likely to the woman who cleans the rooms or the janitor who unplugs the sinks . . . I really wonder if . . . you found Jesus? I know you would try to hide it but I can tell you now, you'll never be successful. I thank God for giving me this opportunity to write you.

A woman from Illinois

I attended a seminary for three years and also have consulted many people, and the more one lives the more one sees and understands there is more to life than just bold scientifically provable or demonstrable things—there is also an eternal spiritual world all around us that can in the person of Jesus or a saint or someone else today. . . break into time and actually *heal—our little time warped minds should not try to limit or deny divinity—so Jesus may also have actually healed or raised from the dead as well as accepted people sociologically back into the community.*

A man from Illinois

I've been working at a VA hospital caring for stroke patients. . . . At night in my emergency room when I meet someone and just see the hurt and the need there, the supernatural, saving Christ image makes me sick, like some type of stupid joke. It's not that I don't believe that the Christian hope voiced in the language of myth, particularly the confession that suffering can be healed, cannot sometimes become real. Personally, I believe that hope for the redemption of our world lies in the extent to which we can share emotional, spiritual, social, and physical healing. The question is not whether suffering can be healed, but how do we induce this healing? How do we help each other become whole? I want to find out.

A woman from Missouri

With all due respect, I would like to suggest that there may be more taking place in those healing stories than you seem to allow:

There may have been real healing of the disease, to borrow a term you use, not just a healing of the illness. . . . Almost all of the healings attributed to Jesus in the canonical Gospels involve what could have been psychosomatic symptoms.

A man from Minnesota

[The possessed woman in the "Overture" to The Historical Jesus: The Life of a Mediterranean Jewish Peasant *had what is] called "clinical depression"—nothing more, nothing less—the most "un" and "mis" diagnosed ailment on our big blue ball. Was it actually around for your basic first-century peasant Jew? Trust me, in big supply. . . . Now just imagine Jesus "itinerating" right across some major boundaries. . . . He passes out the best "healing" that ever was and ever will be—KINDNESS. No big deal huh? Actually, it is still the only universal "treatment.". . . I still say if Jesus [cured in a] trance, how on earth could he ask the rest of us to go and do likewise without giving lessons? Was he asking "all" the others to go do just what he did—or something "kind of" like he did or what? If it factors down to anything less— you've screwed yourself—I say.*

A woman from South Carolina

What about those nature miracles? For example, did Jesus walk on the water or did he not? Did Jesus create a miraculous catch of fishes or did he not?

There is one striking difference between the nature miracles and the healings or exorcisms of Jesus. The nature miracles are performed for the disciples (or mother) of Jesus but the healings or exorcisms are for outsiders. Even the multiplication of loaves and fishes is performed through the disciples, who act as intermediaries in requesting, serving, and clearing the meal. In the two cases mentioned, those miracles are not for ordinary people, but for the official followers of Jesus. Why? Think of the stories once more. The disciples row on the Lake of Galilee without Jesus and get nowhere against the storm. Jesus comes to them walking on the waters; all is immediately safe and well. The disciples fish on the Lake of Galilee without Jesus and catch nothing. Jesus calls to them from the shore; they catch more than they can handle. I consider those twin stories to be clearly symbolic: without Jesus nothing, with Jesus everything. In the boat of the Church it is Jesus who counts and Jesus who is in charge. The disciples even as leaders are totally dependent on Jesus.

But did those who originally wrote those stories intend them to be read literally?

I do not think so. It is not that ancient people told silly stories which we, because we are so smart, should not take literally or factually but symbolically or fictionally. It is the ancients who knew how to tell a good metaphorical story (a parable, if you prefer) and we moderns who are silly enough to take them factually.

I have, of course, not gone into all the so-called nature miracles, but that preceding answer tells you how to generalize about them. The nature miracles are authority parables. They are not about Jesus' power over nature, but about the disciples' authority in the Church. Sorry if that is disappointing, but I insist that to take them literally is to misread them completely.

You made a distinction earlier between nature miracles and human miracles such as Jesus' healings or exorcisms. What about them?

The healings and exorcisms come from a very different viewpoint and they concern outsiders or strangers rather than the insiders or disciples. But allow me a moment of autobiography because my general understanding of God's presence in human history is important here.

I have visited Lourdes in France and Fatima in Portugal, healing shrines of the Christian Virgin Mary. I have also visited Epidaurus in Greece and Pergamum in Turkey, healing shrines of the pagan god Asklepios. The miraculous healings recorded in both places were remarkably the same. There are, for example, many crutches hanging in the grotto of Lourdes, mute witness to those who arrived lame and left whole. There are, however, no prosthetic limbs among them, no witnesses to paraplegics whose lost limbs were restored. What do I conclude?

Faith heals! That is as sure as anything we can ever know. Certain diseases for certain people under certain circumstances can be healed by faith in that very possibility—at Epidaurus for a pagan, at Lourdes for a Christian, at Benares for a Hindu, and so on. But certain diseases only, certain people only, and certain conditions only. And that is exactly what Jesus said again and again: Your faith has healed you. I do not understand that process completely (nor does anyone else) but, leaving aside fakes and charlatans, faith heals—sometimes. Did people come to Jesus to be healed? Absolutely. Were some or even many healed? Absolutely. But there had to be something about Jesus that made people come to him for healing as distinct, say, from John the Baptist to whom they went for baptizing, not healing. That is the question we should probe. Of course certain people were and are healed by their faith in Jesus, but why was it faith in Jesus?

Can you give me a concrete example of how Jesus healed somebody?

Remember the story of the leper. I use it as a case study of what we have been discussing.

First of all, it is important to note that the modern term "leprosy" is flatly wrong as a translation of the Greek word used in this story. That Greek word actually referred to several different skin diseases, all of which involved a rather repulsive scaly or flaking skin condition such as psoriasis, eczema, or fungus infections. So whenever the Bible uses the word "leprosy," it must be understood as referring to those diseases rather than to what we now call "Hansen's disease" or "leprosy."

I don't mean to be rude, but who cares what the ancient disease was? Isn't it really the healing that counts?

Yes and no. Of course the healing of an individual sufferer matters. But what we have in this story goes deeper than that; it is an enacted parable about the society as a whole.

You remember what we were saying earlier: that the table is a miniature model of relationships within the society as a whole. The same thing is true of the individual human body. Anthropologists tell us that *the body is a symbol of the society*; the way one deals with the human body expresses an understanding of social relationships and differences. Every adolescent knows that tattooing arms, coloring hair, piercing anatomy, or adorning the body can either challenge one's group quite fundamentally, or affirm one's group connection. In the 1960s, for example, long hair immediately sent a message about one's attitude toward the established institutions of society. And you won't find dreadlocks in a Marine boot camp. So, when we look at healing stories, we need to be alert to "body image" issues in Jesus' society.

***Yes, but what does that have to do with these skin diseases
that you say are mistranslated as "leprosy"?***

These diseases exactly illustrate the point that the body
becomes a symbol of the whole society. The Jewish state
was a society always threatened with absorption by a more
powerful and imperial culture. In such a situation of political, military, cultural, and religious oppression, an emphasis on protecting *social* boundaries was symbolized by an
emphasis on protecting *bodily* boundaries. So our question
is: When Jesus heals the leper, is he acting only as a healer
of disease or also as a critic of society?

It sounds pretty far-fetched to me.

I don't deny that in these stories we are entering a world
of thought and practice that is very, very strange to us. That
may, indeed, be the beginning of wisdom: to recognize that
the world of the biblical story is, in many ways, not our
world. That recognition will at least keep us from making
gross errors of assuming that we can understand it on twentieth-century terms.

But let me suggest that the sense of the individual body
as a model for the body politic is not so far-fetched after all.
I mentioned that a threatened society, like the Jewish state,
has an intense interest in establishing and protecting
boundaries. One of the ways that this shows up in the law
book called Leviticus is in numerous rules about the body's
openings—about food going into the body, or babies coming out of it. The problem of these diseases lumped together as *leprosy* is that they cause openings to appear on the
skin where they are not meant to be—in other words, all
the boundaries are broken, and the bodily system breaks
down. (In Leviticus, by the way, leprosy applies not only to
skin, but also to clothes and to house walls.) Each surface is

in some circumstances made ritually unclean—that is, socially inappropriate. I realize that this is a very strange way of thinking to the modern mind, but it does help us to see that the person with a skin disease—the "leper"—is a source of social concern, not simply because of medical contagion, as we might imagine, but because of *symbolic contamination*. The breakdown of the boundaries of the body symbolizes a threat to the integrity and security of the society as a whole. That's why in Leviticus 13:45–46 we read:

> *The person who has the leprous disease shall wear torn clothes and let the hair of his head be disheveled; and he shall cover his upper lip and cry out, "Unclean, unclean." He shall remain unclean as long as he has the disease; he is unclean. He shall live alone; his dwelling shall be outside the camp.*

That last line tells us what society's view of the afflicted individual was: "He shall live alone; his dwelling shall be outside the camp." What Jesus did was to welcome the outcast back inside the community from which he had been expelled. That *welcome home* was the healing.

I'm confused. Are you saying that the leper was really healed, or not?

I don't want you to think I'm evading all your tough questions, so let me just say: Yes, he was healed. That being said, bear with me a bit while I make a distinction between *curing a disease* and *healing an illness*.

Studies of many different societies have shown us that disease and illness are not the same thing. Doctors diagnose and treat *diseases*, but patients suffer *illnesses*. To put it bluntly, a disease is something between me, my doctor, and a bug. Something is wrong with my body, and I take it to a doctor to be fixed. And that's important. But there are other dimensions of my experience that are missing from that picture, not just the entire *psychological* meaning of the disease to me, but, much more important, the entire *social* dimension of it. How have I been brought up to think about my body, about modern medicine, about doctors? How does whatever is wrong with me affect my family, my job, or even wider levels of society? *Disease* sees the problem in a narrow, physical focus; *illness* sees it in a wider psychological and social context.

Think, for example, of AIDS. Did you see Tom Hanks's portrayal of an AIDS sufferer in *Philadelphia*? Was his suffering only what was going on in his body's immune system? Or was it also what he experienced in rejection, loss of his job, struggle to find a lawyer? There is a tremendous difference between curing the disease and healing the illness in AIDS. A cure for the disease is absolutely desirable, though not yet discovered; but where we cannot cure the disease, we can still heal the illness—by refusing to ostracize those who have it, by empathizing with their anguish, and by enveloping their suffering with respect and love. That is precisely what Jesus was doing with the leper—welcoming back into social relationship the person who had been an outcast. Jesus healed the illness, rather than the disease. If Jesus were here today, I do not for a moment believe that he could cure the disease known as AIDS, but I am confident that he could heal the illness known by that same name.

So you are saying that Jesus healed the leper, but it was not a miracle?

It all depends on what you mean by miracle. If you mean the use of supernatural power to set aside the usual workings of the natural world, then, no, it was not a miracle.

And it certainly was not—as is sometimes claimed—a proof of Jesus' divinity, since he told his followers to do precisely the same thing. Jesus, in my view, was not curing a disease through an intervention in the physical world, but was healing the illness through an intervention in the social world. He healed by refusing to buy into the customary sanctions against diseased persons. Jesus healed the "leper" by inviting him back into human community, that ideal human community called the Kingdom of God. He refused to accept the disease as ritual uncleanness, thereby forcing others either to accept the leper back into the community or to reject Jesus from it as well. The power of healing is a gift of God built permanently into the fabric of the universe, not just a temporary or periodic intervention of God into a closed universe which lacks such possibility.

There is one more aspect of the story that I ask you to notice. In inviting the leper back into the community of God's people, Jesus was issuing a challenge to those who were the society's boundary keepers. He offered himself as an alternative boundary keeper in a way that was quite rightly seen as subversive to the established procedures of his society. His *welcome home* to the leper put him on a direct collision course with the priestly authorities in the Temple who had charge of such boundary situations. Mark captured that original meaning in his closing comment, ascribed to Jesus, that the leper should go to the priest "as a testimony to them." That phrase might be better translated "as a witness against them"—in other words, "as a challenge to them." Perhaps it does seem to some that such an interpretation destroys the miracle. But I believe that miracles are not changes in the physical world so much as changes in the social world. It would, of course, be nice to have certain miracles available to change the physical world if we could, but it seems to me much more desirable to make certain changes which lie within our power in the social world.

If you have found it tough going to enter into the mental world of the healing of the leper, the going is about to get tougher still. We need also to deal with the fact that the historical Jesus is undeniably portrayed to us as an *exorcist*, casting out demons.

Jesus, an exorcist? Are we seriously to believe in demon possession, let alone that Jesus cast demons out?

Unquestionably, talk about *demons* and *unclean spirits* is weird to us. Let me say at the outset that I, myself, do not believe that there are personal, supernatural spirits who invade our bodies and, for either good or evil, jostle for control with our own personality. But the vast majority of the world's people have so believed, and according to one recent survey, about seventy-five percent of the human population still believes in such spirit possession. So we have to ask some difficult questions. What is it they are seeing, and why are they seeing it that way? Are we seeing something completely different, or the same phenomena through different eyes? I'm sure, in any case, that we haven't explained anything by simply saying, "I don't believe in demons." We may not have the same diagnosis, but that doesn't mean there are no symptoms to explain. On the other hand, it does make a difference what form of explanation we use. Let me illustrate that with two examples.

One psychiatrist tells the story of Mary, a thirteen year-old girl on the Yakima Indian Reservation in central Washington. A local medical doctor had diagnosed her hysterical symptoms as paranoid schizophrenia and prescribed a potent drug. The psychiatrist, however, was sensitive to the girl's culture. He learned that her dying shaman grandfather had prophesied that his power would descend to her, but that she herself wanted to become a part of the majority

American society. Since the psychological conflict was rooted in a sense of unwanted shamanistic spirits, he advised a
native ceremony of exorcism. After that ceremony the girl
recovered completely. In her culture of origin that ritual
made sense and was therefore effective.

On the other hand, I recall an exorcism ritual that was
shown on prime time American television a few years ago.
Those involved in the ritual all believed that the young girl
was possessed, and when the priest came away from con-
fronting the screaming, cursing patient, he announced that
he had looked into the face of evil. But does the category of
demon possession prove most fruitful for understanding that
case? If, for example, some type of multiple personality disorder was hidden behind that supposed demon possession,
the face of evil might be, in fact, sitting in the next room in
the form of, say, an older male who had sexually abused the
girl in infancy and shattered her unformed personality into
defensive shreds. Calling her *demon possessed* implies blame
for the victim, who must surely have done something to
have caused such a fate. Would it not make more sense to
use the contemporary diagnosis of multiple personality disorder, which involves no further victimizing of the victim?
In other words, *names matter*. It may not make any sense at
all to take categories of demon possession and exorcism
into our contemporary world. But it makes a great deal of
sense to ask what those words meant (and sometimes still
mean) in other cultures.

Recall one of the biblical stories of exorcism. Mark
(5:1–17) tells us that Jesus once came to the country of the
Gerasenes. There he met a man with an *unclean spirit* who
lived amongst the tombs, so powerful that no one could
bind him, even with chains. He was always crying out and
bruising himself with stones. When he saw Jesus, he yelled,
"What have you to do with me, Jesus, Son of the Most
High God? Do not torment me." Jesus asked him what at
first may seem to be a strange question, "What is your

name?" He answered, "My name is Legion; for we are many." Then we are told that the demons begged Jesus to send them out of the man into a herd of pigs feeding on the hillside, and Jesus gave them permission to go, after which about two thousand pigs rushed down a bank into the sea and were drowned. People from the surrounding country-side came to see what had happened, found the man who had been possessed by demons now calm, clothed, and in his right mind. And the story concludes, "They began to beg Jesus to depart from their neighborhood."

Let me be clear that I do not regard this as an actual scene from the life of the historical Jesus. Though Jesus' exorcisms are often mentioned in the gospels, we have no example of *particular stories* that are verified by more than one source. What seems to have happened is that the general tradition of Jesus as an exorcist eventually led to invented stories about what that ministry looked like. And so the question we need to ask about this particular story is: What do we see in it? What seems to be going on?

Well for one thing I see a rather shocking indifference on Jesus' part to other people's property! Seriously, it just comes across to me as a bizarre story with no redeeming social significance.

It's strange, all right. But in light of the studies I mentioned earlier that show the individual body to be a symbol of the whole society, take a look at two of its features. First, when asked his name, the possessed man replies, "My name is *Legion*." The Legion, of course, is a unit of Roman military power and symbolizes the oppressive overlord of the Jewish homeland. That power is cast out into the most impure of Judaism's ritually unclean animals, and then (and this is the second feature I want you to notice) the Legion is *cast into the sea and drowned*. Who can possibly miss that most fervent dream of every Jewish freedom fighter—that the Romans be pushed back into the Mediterranean Sea?

There is a close connection between *possession* and *oppression*, whether the subjugation be the sexual one of women by men, or the racial and imperial one of some people by other people. An occupied country has, as it were, a multiple personality disorder. One part of it hates and despises the oppressor, but the other part envies and admires its superior power. And if the body is a symbol of the society, certain individuals may well experience exactly the same split within themselves. In the first-century mind, I am arguing, there was a connection between demonic possession and colonial oppression.

Isn't it possible that as a twentieth-century scholar you are simply reading back your understanding into first-century minds?

We always have to be careful that we do not simply retroject contemporary concerns into ancient minds, but let me give you an example that helps persuade me that it is not so in this case. The story concerns the Lunda-Luvale tribes of what used to be northern Rhodesia. According to one scholar they had traditional ailments resulting from possession by ancestral spirits that were called "*mahamba*." But then they developed a special modern affliction called "*bindele*," which is their word for "European." This new ailment required for its healing a special exorcistic church and a lengthy curative process. It seems to me that the *Legion* of Mark's story was to colonial Roman Palestine as *bindele* was to colonial European Rhodesia. In both cases colonial exploitation took on bodily form as demonic possession. When, therefore, Jesus exorcises, he is not simply healing individuals, but is engaging in symbolic revolution against the occupying power.

You haven't said much about how Jesus healed—in this case, how he "cast out demons."

It's a good question and, of course, extremely difficult to answer.

We know that in every culture are found altered states of consciousness and that these states are frequently used in healing. This is particularly true of premodern cultures with far less capacity to cure diseases than to heal illnesses. Native healers in many cultures have entered into trance states—altered states of consciousness—or produced such states in their patients as part of the healing process. In the modern world, physicians and psychologists use heightened suggestibility in patients as part of the healing process—as is most clearly evidenced in hypnosis.

It is in this context that I want to take a brief look at an incident where Jesus is attacked by his critics (Luke 11:14–15):

> *Now he was casting out a demon that was dumb; when the demon had gone out, the dumb man spoke, and the people marveled. But some of them said, "He casts out demons by Beelzebul, the prince of demons."*

Beelzebul, the name of an ancient Canaanite god, is here a symbol for Satan. You might again say that we have here simply a case of name-calling. But as with those accusations we mentioned earlier of gluttony and drunkenness, perhaps the name-calling is based on something that makes the naming at least possibly believable.

The question raised in my mind is whether Jesus himself sometimes healed while in an altered state of consciousness or trance. I am fully aware that there is not much evidence for Jesus as an entranced healer using contagious trance as a therapeutic technique. But I am also aware that the talky, preachy, speechy side of religion is also not too much at home with the touchy, feely, squealy side. So it is at least possible that the tradition ignored this side of Jesus even if it was present there originally. I realize that my suggestion is speculative, but I just want to leave the question open for the future. This much is certain—and it is my bottom line—that Jesus not only *discussed* the Kingdom of God, but *enacted* it, and that enacting meant healing people in a context that posed a challenge to both social authorities and imperial power.

Let me ask you a general question about miracles before we talk about Jesus. Do you believe in miracles then or now, ever or never?

Recall my earlier distinction between statements of fact and statements of faith. I apply it now to the distinction between marvel and miracle. A marvel is something for which I or we have no adequate explanation at the moment. And there are far more marvels around than we usually admit. I do not believe we live in a closed universe where we understand everything completely; and even if we understood the world completely, it would still be *our* understanding. So I expect to find multitudes of things I cannot understand or explain, what TV programs like to call mysteries and what I call marvels or wonders or puzzles. What is objectively present is a marvel, something we wonder about because we have no adequate explanation. When people declare that a marvel is a miracle, they are making an act of faith, they are declaring that, *for them*, God has acted directly and immediately in this situation, God has intervened outside normal, regular, or natural processes to create that marvel. That is, by definition, an act of faith, an ultimate interpretation beyond proof or disproof. There could not be an objective miracle unless we lived in an absolutely closed universe, all of whose processes and laws we understood. Then anything inexplicable would be a miracle, an intrusion of the supernatural into the closed system of the natural world.

But, granted that to declare a miracle is to make an act of faith, do you yourself believe in miracles?

Yes, but not as periodic intrusions in some closed natural order. I leave absolutely open what God *could* do, but I have very definite thoughts about what God *does* do. The supernatural or divine is not something that periodically or temporarily breaks through the normal surface of the natural or human world. The supernatural is more like the permanently hidden but perpetually beating heart of the natural. It is always there for those with spirit to see or faith to hear. And, if every now and then, somebody sees an inbreaking presence here or there, I do not mock that claim because I understand those experiences as subjectively read signs of that abiding presence. What is seriously wrong for me is to discern the holy only in the cracks and fissures of the natural order rather than everywhere present over, under, around, and through that natural order. I believe, then, in miracles as the places where individuals or groups see God at work. Jesus is, for me, a miracle.

Is that a prejudice against miracles that invalidates your reading of gospel claims about Jesus?

First of all, everyone draws a line of credibility somewhere. Every time I stand at the grocery check out I find myself confronted with weekly tabloids announcing gossip, scandal, and miracle. I do not believe any of them and if that's prejudice, so be it. Second, I presume natural consistency. When Aesop has animals talk I do not presume that animals spoke in ancient Greece nor that ancient Greeks believed they did. A standard presumption of natural consistency helps me identify the literary style of fable in which important moral lessons come disguised as talking animal tales. Aesop is a warning; if you take him literally you misunderstand him badly. I call that the "Aesop Fallacy" and it is far too prevalent in reading the Bible. Third, I also presume divine consistency: what God does now is what God always did. God "intervened" no more and no less in the world of the early first century than that of the late twentieth century. These are presuppositions or, if you prefer, prejudices, but so, of course, are the opposite opinions.

You said earlier that the healings of the pagan Greek god Asklepios and the Christian Virgin Mary are very similar to one another and to the miracles of Jesus. But what about those stories that Jesus raised people from the dead? What about Lazarus? Did those really happen?

It is interesting how densely the symbolic dimension surrounds a story like Lazarus. Here is a key section of the story:

Martha said to Jesus, "Lord, if you had been here, my brother would not have died. And even now I know that whatever you ask from God, God will give you." Jesus said to her, "Your brother will rise again." Martha said to him, "I know that he will rise again in the resurrection at the last day." Jesus said to her, "I am the resurrection and the life; he who believes in me, though he die, yet shall he live, and whoever lives and believes in me shall never die. Do you believe this?" She said to him, "Yes, Lord; I believe that you are the Christ, the Son of God, he who is coming into the world." (John 11:21–27)

How shall we understand this story? In terms of divine consistency, I do not think that anyone, anywhere, at any time, including Jesus, brings dead people back to life. (I am not, of course, talking about near-death experiences or about resuscitating apparent corpses. Death means you don't come back. If you come back, it was not death. Death, like pregnancy, is either/or, not more or less.) But I think I can see what is happening in this story, which in a very profound sense is true.

To take an example from our own society, suppose that you stood in front of a "Lincoln High School" somewhere in Midwest America. And suppose that in front of that school you saw a statue of Lincoln with upraised ax ready to smash through the chains binding a slave's feet. My question to you is: Is that true or false? Well, of course, no such event ever happened, yet that nonevent *symbolizes* the whole course and meaning of Lincoln's life. Might we not say that the symbolism involved in that statue is *true* even though no such event actually occurred?

That's what I think is going on in these stories of raising the dead. In John's gospel the event of Lazarus' restoration illustrates the general resurrection of the dead, an event in the distant future. But I can imagine peasants all over lower Galilee who would have said with equal intensity that Jesus brought life out of death for them right here and now in this present life. *Life out of death is how they would have understood their experience of the Kingdom of God* in which they began to take back control over their own bodies, their own hopes, and their own destinies. Jesus said that the Kingdom of God, the will of God for earth, was not Caesar's way; that it was diametrically opposed to Caesar's way; that it was the opposite of occupation and collaboration, oppression and domination, discrimination and marginalization. Such a claim was the first and most basic act of social healing, healing on the ideological level without which healing can never occur on any other level. His hearers who experienced the Kingdom of God's empowering presence knew that it meant life out of death; to have Jesus knock on the door of a tomb was an obvious parable for that experience. It was a dramatic video-bite, so to speak, for a much larger process.

My point, once again, is *not* that those ancient people told literal stories and we are now smart enough to take them symbolically, but that they told them symbolically and we are now dumb enough to take them literally. They knew what they were doing; we don't.

One final point connected with those healings. Why does Jesus seem always on the move? As soon as he heals somebody, he hurries off somewhere else.

I think that picturing Jesus as always going somewhere rather than being settled in one place is thereby interpreting what his ministry is about.

Let me get at this by noting an interesting problem in New Testament study. We are told in Mark (6:4) that Jesus' own family did not believe in him. Yet when Paul arrived in Jerusalem, say, around the year 38, he found James, the *brother* of Jesus, already there, along with Peter and in a position of authority. So we have a problem. What happened in between? How did James get from disbelief to belief and from Nazareth to Jerusalem? What I suggest is that Jesus' family did, in fact, believe in his power and mission but not at all in the way he was carrying it out.

In Mediterranean culture, relationships were governed by patron/client ties. Remember that there was a very small upper class and a very large lower class. What kept society together were multiple ties between patrons and clients. Those without power could be clients to the patrons above them, and those patrons might be clients to others far more powerful still. Brokers were clients to those above them and patrons to those below. The system, at its best, gave some hope for recognition to lower class individuals but, at its worst, confirmed their dependency and oppression. I believe that the problem Jesus' family had with him was that they wanted him to settle down at his home in Nazareth and establish there a healing cult. He would be its *patron*, the family would be its *brokers*, and as his reputation went out along the peasant grapevine, the sick would come as *clients* to be healed. That would have been good for everyone. But instead Jesus kept to the road, brought healing to those who needed it, and, as it were, started anew every day. That was no way to run a healing ministry and no way to treat his family—especially in the world of Mediterranean values. So it's not surprising that once Jesus was gone, we find his brother James firmly settled, precisely located in Jerusalem—and in charge.

We have another story that throws light on why Jesus kept moving (Mark 1:35–38). He entered Peter's house, healed Peter's mother-in-law, and the town's sick people gathered for healing at Peter's door. Any Mediterranean person would know that Peter's house was becoming a brokerage place for Jesus' healing. But Jesus went out the next morning to a lonely place to pray, and when Peter caught up to him to take him back, Jesus said, "Let us go on to the next towns, that I may preach there also; for that is why I came out."

Mark created that story to show Jesus opposing Peter, because from Mark's point of view, they had different visions of mission. Peter was ready to have Jesus settle down and to broker his patronage to sick clients. Jesus was ready to move on because he offered an *unbrokered Kingdom* to all who needed him. The equal sharing of spiritual and material gifts, of miracle and table, cannot be centered in one place because that very hierarchy of place, of here above there, of this place above other places, symbolically destroys the radically open community it announces. For Jesus the Kingdom of God is not his to offer as patron or for others to broker. The Kingdom of God is a community of radical or unbrokered equality in which individuals are in direct contact with one another and with God, unmediated by any established brokers and fixed locations.

6

Did Jesus Intend to Start a New Religion?

As an agnostic Jew, please know that I stand in awe of the universe and the laws of nature. Where and how it all started is surely beyond our present knowledge and maybe beyond any expectation of ever knowing. Meanwhile, I suggest that human progress will always be dependent on people like yourself who are not beholden to rigid orthodoxy—and with the courage to stand up.
A man from Illinois

We both embrace and mourn the demythologizing of so very much of our Christian tradition [in Jesus: A Revolutionary Biography*]. At one point one of us said, "He's taken away Christmas, he's taken away the miracles and now he's taking away Easter as well." We cannot help wondering if the glorious music and art these tales have inspired would have resulted if those Biblical passages had been seen as just "stories." However, we are also aware that you haven't really taken them away. In some sense it is possible to embrace their truth more fully now that the stories are not burdened with a literalism they cannot sustain.*
A group in Ohio

Most of us have not thought of Jesus as a peasant leading—in effect—a social revolution. This vision of Jesus covers equality, justice, non-discrimination, healing and management power. Yes, we know this is the work of Christianity, but how often do we think of Jesus "leading the charge."
A woman from Illinois

*With all sincerity we would like for you to consider the follow-
ing questions: Were you alive when Jesus performed his ministry?
Were you present at his crucifixion and burial? Were you present
at his resurrection? If you were not, how can you consider yourself to be an authority on what took place and why it took place?
. . . We do not consider ourselves to be authorities, but we believe
in his physical resurrection as witnessed by many who were there.*

                                                    A group from Illinois

*If Jesus as the rural, Jewish version of the philosophical Cynic
School is a personal model, how can we authentically have possessions, live in relative comfort, hold steady institutional jobs, and
get married?*

                                                    A man from Arizona

*Through my high school and particularly my college years . . .
I just could not accept so much of the mythology surrounding the
gospels and the life of Jesus that I heard in church. . . . The two
books of yours fulfill the need of mine to find out what the real
Jesus taught and lived. l was absolutely fascinated and couldn't
put them down. . . . After reading the books, I am struck by the
fact that the real message of Jesus is probably the hardest one to
really follow and live, that is, opening one's heart to society's outcasts, healing and eating with people who have little or nothing
of material wealth. But at least now, my soul tells me I'm on the
right track.*

                                                    A man from Virginia

**Did Jesus intend to found a new religion, the one we now
call Christianity, or at least to create a separate Christian
church?**

The answer to that is an emphatic no, but that does not
mean Jesus did not have a very specific program. He was
more than just a visionary with an idea about God. He also

intended to assist others in living the life demanded by that God. Jesus' intention was to restore a peasant community that was under acute strain from Roman colonization and urbanization. He did that by announcing a divine ideal, a God of radical justice in a kingdom of utter equality. I take your question to ask whether Jesus had a monopoly on that kingdom or whether it entailed a social program available to all who wanted to participate in its presence.

I have emphasized throughout this book that Jesus came from a peasant class. It now becomes important to take a closer look at what that means in terms of Jesus' mission as a program.

We need to begin by recognizing that peasant classes—particularly, as in first-century Palestine, when under the heel of an oppressive power—must make critical decisions about how to resist. And resist they will—in one way or another. Anthropologists distinguish between open or extraordinary and hidden or ordinary forms of peasant resistance. We tend to think only of *overt* resistance appearing in such actions as revolt or rebellion. But these are usually last-ditch desperate efforts and usually doomed to disastrous failure. There is also, however, *covert* resistance, that everyday reaction which stays just below the surface and cannot therefore be so easily detected, readily punished, or effectively eliminated. Everything from minor sabotage, theft, or arson, to acting dumb, making mistakes, or misunderstanding orders constitute the everyday and ordinary forms of protest which maintain the dignity of the oppressed without inviting lethal punishment.

That distinction helps us sort out peasant responses to Roman rule in the first-century Jewish homeland. There, as elsewhere, resistance did not usually begin with outright revolt—although that is often the point where oppressors first noticed the problem. Certainly there were *overt* forms of resistance: unarmed protesters, armed bandits, apocalyptic prophets, and messianic leaders. We have detailed descriptions of such forms of resistance and revolt from the aristocratic historian Josephus—because such elite observers pay attention to open and obvious forms of resistance. But *overt* resistance is always only the tip of the iceberg of peasant unrest. Most of that unrest is *covert*, hidden below the surface, and not visible to the powers against which it is aimed.

Perhaps I may use an illustration from my own background. The story presumes, centuries before, the exile of the Irish aristocracy and its replacement by British elites. A lost English huntsman in late-nineteenth-century Donegal asks an Irish peasant, "Did the gentry pass this way, my good man?" "They did that, your honor." "How long ago?" "About three hundred years ago, your honor." That is an example of a very small, relatively safe act of resistance— repeatable as story over and over again.

My argument about the mission of Jesus is this: That *what he was doing was located exactly on the borderline between overt and covert resistance*. On the one hand, his resistance was not as overt as that of protesters, prophets, bandits, or messiahs. On the other hand, it was far more overt than merely playing dumb, imagining revenge, or retelling stories from the times of Moses or David. His open eating and free healing were at the precise borderline between covert and overt, secret and open, private and public resistance. But I insist that it was nonetheless a mission of resistance.

Was that resistance, in your opinion, a purely personal response on Jesus' part, or was he trying to organize a social movement? Did he try to enlist other people in his mission?

I can accept the term "mission" to describe what Jesus was up to because it was more than merely a personal lifestyle. Of course, I don't mean to read into the word "mission" the whole enterprise, for example, of Paul's journeys throughout the Mediterranean world, much less any theology of later Christian evangelizing. But it is clear to me that Jesus had a magnificent vision of the Kingdom of God here on earth and lived that vision out. What is clear to me also is that he *empowered other persons* to be actively involved with him in that mission. You remember how John the Baptist organized a community of the baptized spread out across the Jewish homeland waiting for the action of the avenging God. I think that Jesus also was organizing a movement—but with a very different message from a very different God. Call it a companionship of empowerment.

Can you say briefly what that mission was?

I have already described Jesus' practice of an open table and free healing. I think his mission was basically this: to invite others into that style of life as a challenge and empowerment. The heart of the original Jesus movement was sharing an open table and offering free healing. That combination of shared material resources (eating) and shared spiritual resources (healing) is absolutely at the core of Jesus' mission. That process involved a radically different spirituality. It sought to bring individuals together into a community which experienced God in that companionship, but not just through that companionship. Instead of the hierarchy of patrons and brokers, mediators and intermediaries which structured Mediterranean society and religion, Jesus lived an open and direct relationship with God and invited others to do likewise. The Kingdom of God was not a program for isolated individuals; it was for communal life empowering participants into direct contact with God rather than becoming itself a substitute for that challenge.

Take a look with me at one of the major texts referring to this mission:

[Jesus] said, "The harvest is abundant, but the workers are few; beg therefore the master of the harvest to send our workers into his harvest. Go. Look, I send you out as lambs among wolves. Do not carry money, or bag, or sandals, [or staff]; and do not greet anyone on the road.

"Whatever house you enter, say, 'Peace be to this house.' And if a child of peace is there, your peace will rest upon him. But if not, let your peace return to you. And stay in the same house, eating and drinking *whatever they pro-vide, for the worker deserves his wages [in Luke; but in Matthew: food]. Do not go from house to house.*

"And if you enter a town and they receive you, eat what is set before you. *Heal the sick and say to them 'God's kingdom has come near to you.' But if you enter a town and they do not receive you, as you leave, shake the dust from your feet and say, 'Nevertheless, be sure of this, the realm of God has come to you.' (Luke 10:2–11, emphasis added)*

There are several questions we need to ask about this text. The first is: Who is Jesus sending out on this mission? The *Gospel of Thomas* simply says "followers"; the *Q Gospel* refers to "seventy others"; and Mark refers to "the twelve apostles." My answer to our question is that those whom Jesus sent out were not from a specific, closed group. But they were probably not so much those who had voluntarily given up everything as those who had recently lost every-thing. They were located along that terrible divide between poverty and destitution. It was there that the processes of Roman urbanization pressed most heavily on the peasantry. Not every peasant was becoming destitute, but peasant life was becoming very insecure and unstable. I suggest, in other words, that Jesus created a *network of shared apocalyptic heal-ing* just as John had created a network of shared expectation.

There is one special point I want to make in this discussion of the "who." When Mark tells the story, he has Jesus send-ing out the Twelve, *two by two*. We need to ask why. If I may look ahead to a highly symbolic story that we will study more closely in the chapter on Easter—the Emmaus Road story—we may find a clue to the meaning of missionaries in pairs. In that story two followers of Jesus traveled from Jerusalem to Emmaus on Easter Sunday. One of them is given a name, Cleopas, a male. The other person is left unnamed. With any such pair in Mediterranean society, when the first person is named (male) and the second is unnamed, we may assume that the second person is a *woman*. Notice, however, that she is not identified as being Cleopas' wife. How are we to understand this pairing?

When Paul is discussing his own missionary activities (l Corinthians 9:5), he writes: "Do we not have the right to be accompanied by a believing wife, as do the other apostles and the brothers of the Lord and Cephas?"

The literal meaning in the Greek language, "sister wife," was translated into English as "believing wife."

But Paul was, in fact, unmarried. My proposal is that "sister wife" refers not to a partner in marriage, but to a female missionary who travels with a male missionary as if, for the world at large, she is his wife. Why this pairing? The obvious answer is that it would provide social protection for a traveling female missionary in a world of male power and violence. I suggest that was the original purpose of Jesus' sending missionaries out in pairs—namely, to allow for female missionaries. That male/female partnership in mission has obvious significance, not only for understanding Jesus' intention, but also for the role of women in modern Christianity.

Part of that mission passage quoted above is here worth a careful look: "Do not carry money, or bag, or sandals [or staff]; and do not greet anyone on the road." This is a picture of what you might call "the dress code" of the Kingdom movement.

A dress code for the Kingdom of God?

Actually, yes—and a fairly strict one at that. But the point, of course, is the symbolism of the dress code. In fact, as you read later versions of this story (for example, in the gospel of Mark), you'll find that this more radical dress code is made more lenient. Whereas here the missionaries are told not to carry money, or bag, or sandals, or staff, Mark *allows* them to carry a staff and sandals. Wherever we see more stringent or radical requirements being watered down, we may be confident that time has passed and the Church is adjusting the lifestyle of the historical Jesus to its own later needs. So I conclude that the forbidding of purse, bag, sandals, staff, and greetings are basic and original, coming from Jesus himself.

What was Jesus' point in making such strict rules about dress and behavior on the road?

To get some clues, let me take you around the Mediterranean Sea for a look at other radical first-century missionaries who, like Jesus, preached to ordinary people both by what they said and how they lived, by what they taught and how they dressed. I refer to the philosophical movement called Cynicism.

Nowadays we use the word "cynicism" to mean belief in nothing or doubt about everything. What it meant in the first century was not simply philosophical disbelief, but also a practical resistance to ordinary cultural values. The Cynics tried to find happiness through freedom from desires, emotions, controls, authorities, public opinion, property, family life. Their symbolic dress code involved carrying a knapsack, holding a staff, and wearing a dirty, ragged cloak which left the right shoulder bare. They usually did not wear shoes and their hair and beards were long and disheveled. You would not be far wrong to see here a picture of first-century *hippies*, dramatizing in dress their refusal to accept society's material values. Cynicism was thus a resistance movement against conventional society— and particularly involved a questioning of power, rule, dominion, and kingship. You may remember the famous story in which the Cynic Diogenes, invited by Alexander the Great to name anything he wanted, asked the conqueror simply to get out of his sunlight. That famous story raises the question: Who is the true ruler, the one who wants everything or the one who needs nothing? Who is really wealthy: the one who wants all of Asia or the one content with just a little sunlight? The Cynics, whose life and dress were a form of street theater among the ordinary people, thus profoundly questioned the assumptions of their culture and, indeed, of civilization.

But if the Cynics around the Mediterranean sound something like the Jesus movement—both agree about wearing no sandals and spending no time on ordinary greetings and gossip along the road—they also have some flat-out disagreements. And here we need especially to talk about wallet and staff.

Actually that term "wallet" is an unfortunate translation, since for us it connotes money. The Greek word would be better translated as "knapsack." What it symbolized for the Cynics was their complete self-sufficiency; that is, they carried their homes and possessions with them. All they need-ed could be carried in a simple knapsack slung over the shoulder. So also with the staff. It represented their itiner-ant status, the fact that they were always spiritually on the way elsewhere. So knapsack and staff symbolized their itin-erant self-sufficiency.

By contrast, the Jesus missionaries are told precisely to carry *no* knapsack and hold *no* staff in their hands. This is a striking difference, and we need to ask what it means. I think it means this: whereas the Cynics are emphasizing *self-sufficiency*, the Jesus missionaries are emphasizing *communal dependency*. The Cynics need no one and nothing; the Jesus missionaries need their food and lodging from others with whom they share the open table and free healing. Both groups are itinerant, but whereas the Cynics are self-sufficient loners, the missionaries sent out by Jesus are dependent upon a new community.

Are you suggesting that Jesus adopted some of his ideas from the Cynic movement?

We really have no way of knowing whether Jesus had even heard about the Cynic movement. The point I'm making is not that Jesus either borrowed from or imitated that movement, but that it's instructive to see how both Jesus and the Cynic preachers appealed to the ordinary people. Both were lifestyle preachers advocating their positions not only by word, but by deed; both symbolized their messages dramatically by dress; both Jesus and the Cynics taught and acted against materialism, oppression, and a distorted sense of what made for real power in the first century. The differences, of course, are also striking. The Cynic was urban, while Jesus was rural; the Cynic followed an individual philosophy of self-sufficiency, while Jesus organized a communal movement; Cynic symbolism demanded knapsack and staff, that of Jesus no knapsack and no staff. Perhaps it is not too much to say that Jesus is what peasant Jewish Cynicism might have looked like. In any case, and even if Jesus had never heard of the Cynics, the comparison helps me understand the meaning of that dress code.

Can you explain more fully that combination of free healing and open eating?

What I see is an interaction between the itinerant missionaries whom Jesus sends out and the householders who receive them into their homes. I think of Jesus' program as a peasant movement aimed precisely at the frightening line between the destitute and the poor, between those who had lost their land and those who were still managing a subsistence living on it. The background to such debt foreclosure, land loss, and impoverishment was, of course, the booming economy of the early first century's *Pax Romana*. This showed up in Lower Galilee as two new walled cities of about twenty-five thousand inhabitants each, one rebuilt after destruction (Sepphoris) and another built from scratch (Tiberias) within twenty years and twenty miles of one another in the first twenty years of Jesus' life. Imagine what those cities did to peasant life and land in the surrounding countryside. Itinerants and householders were often just steps apart, on either side of that terrible line (as some of our American homed and homeless are today).

Jesus' program attempted to rebuild peasant life from its grass roots upwards by bringing those two classes, the destitute and the poor, more even than the poor and the rich, into interaction with each other. The Kingdom of God appears in that interaction because it resides, not just with the itinerants, but with the relationship between itinerants and householders. One group, the itinerants, must move beyond envy and hate; the other group, the householders, must move beyond fear and terror. One needs eating, the other healing; and at a certain point, eating and healing become one.

What about us? To be a real Christian, are we also supposed to adopt a counter-culture, itinerant lifestyle? That doesn't seem very practical.

Good question. Think back to that distinction between *itinerants* and *householders*. When the itinerant missionaries come into a village and accept hospitality from the more settled householders, the householders are not told just to drop everything and hit the road. After all, the message of the itinerants is, "The Kingdom of God has come to you." The householders, too, experience the Kingdom as shared eating and healing *right where they are*.

Very early on, we can sense some tension between the itinerants and the householders. A first-century document called the *Didache* (the word means "teaching") expresses the viewpoint of the householders. They're told, for example: "Do not judge the prophets (i.e. the itinerants), but do not imitate them either." It's okay to live out the Kingdom vision in your village. And they're also told, "if you can bear the whole yoke of the Lord, you will be perfect, but if you cannot, do what you can."

"*Do what you can.*" I think that is an important part of the answer to your question. To be a Christian is to live in the tension between Jesus' radical message/lifestyle and the requirements of daily life for most of us. Meeting Jesus is a little bit like watching Michael Jordan play basketball. You're probably not going to be a Michael Jordan, but you see in him amazing possibilities for the human body—and maybe you start treating your own more respectfully. In a similar way, in Jesus we see new possibilities for human living. When we take him seriously, we live in a creative tension between the requirements of our usual life (like settled householders) and the radical challenge of living counter-culturally (like the itinerants on the road). I think also of a Washington, D.C., activist working on the overwhelming problem of world hunger. Someone asked him how he keeps at it without throwing in the towel and giving up. "You have to have two things," he answered. "One is a vision. The second is an ability to celebrate small victories." That's not a bad way to express the tension between the ideal and present reality. Like those for whom the *Didache* was written, we who have to go to work from eight o'clock to five o'clock, change dirty diapers, and pay the orthodontist, need to hear this message: "Do what you can."

Before we leave the subject of Jesus' missionary movement, I want to call your attention once again to the passage in which the missionaries are sent out. You may have noticed that Luke says, ". . . and stay in the same house, eating and drinking whatever they provide *for the worker deserves his wages*"; in Matthew's version it is "the worker deserves his *food*." I think that something important is at stake in this difference between *food* and *wages*.

What we have here is a transition from food in the context of the open table to food as payment. It seems to be a development that occurred as the Jesus movement became more institutionalized—and perhaps the shift was necessary. But if the mission was becoming more efficient, better organized, and more adapted to urban rather than rural realities, it was also becoming a different mission in the process. What I argue is that the open table was not for Jesus merely a strategy for supporting the mission, a way of "paying" those sent out. The open table was, rather, a strategy for building peasant community at the grassroots level. For that reason any move from *food shared* to *wages due* was a momentous step in the movement's development. It was a step from new community to institution, from movement to church.

7

Who Executed Jesus and Why?

I write to express to you my grateful thanks for your excellent and most readable research and books into the historical Jesus. I have found them to be exciting, challenging and revealing. I have "grown" as a minister of the Church of Scotland through these works.

A man from Scotland

I hope others tell you that your effort to be both scholarly and honest is greatly admirable. I very much appreciate your writing and courage. I hope the critical voices do not inhibit you. I could not put down Jesus: A Revolutionary Biography *until I finished it. Too few are able to sit with and work through the moral clash (between the historian and the believer). But for those who can, please press on. As an Episcopal priest I have long felt alone in an unthinking world. I do not feel so alone now. Thank you very much.*

A man from Illinois

I love to go to the Carmelite Convent to pray but what would they think if they knew that I don't believe Jesus is the only Son of God (if he is, then who am I? Adopted from the Martians, maybe?) And I don't believe that God asked anyone to suffer a cruel, cruel, violent death for me or anyone so that he could be expiated.

A woman from Illinois

I want you to know that your book The Historical Jesus: The Life of a Mediterranean Jewish Peasant . . . *set me on a quest. . . . As one well on the road to the Episcopal priesthood I have spent countless sleepless hours attempting to reach some rational resolve to how best to balance the highly Eucharistic and liturgical creeds and other expressions of our faith in light of all that "higher criticism" and Christology would cast into doubt. Today I finished your* Four Other Gospels. *Where do I find the continuity and the way to understand the juncture between faith and reason, historicity and ecclesiology?*

A man from Georgia

God sent Him as a sacrifice for all sin—once and for all—so that sinful man need not go once a year to give animals' blood for their sins—Also because of his coming into the world, anyone and everyone could be saved from the death that Adam and Eve caused to be brought upon mankind.

A woman from North Carolina

A few months ago I was asked to address a study class in a local Lutheran church. . . . I asked the group, "Why was Jesus killed?" After a long pause, one of the few men in attendance said "So that we can be saved." I replied, "No, that wasn't the reason. He was killed because he was a troublemaker, a rabble-rouser. He was threatening the authority and the income of the existing clergy and government leaders."

A woman form Pennsylvania

You said Jesus taught radical egalitarianism and demanded itinerancy. As to social and political equality no he didn't. In the 17th chapter of John, Jesus plainly stated his kingdom was no part of this world. He refused kingship. That is one reason why the Romans hated the Jews. The Jews claimed that Jesus would rule this earth from Jerusalem. That claim proved false just as it does today. The kingdom is heavenly and it is ruling now!! Soon now your religion and all others except one will be destroyed.

A man from Canada

I think that the members of the Jesus Seminar should realize the seriousness of "peeling away" the New Testament. The Bible is planned out in such a wonderful way that everything fits together perfectly, New Testament and Old Testament alike. God has a special purpose for every single verse in the Bible so I think every verse should remain how it is. I did not write this letter to scold or offend anyone. I did write it to tell you that Jesus Christ died on the cross to bring people close to God again. Immanuel means "God with us." No matter what any historical facts or experts say, I know this is true because He is with me right now as my savior and closest friend.

A woman from Michigan

What was crucifixion and why did people get crucified in the ancient world?

That Jesus "was crucified under Pontius Pilate," as the creed states, is as certain as anything historical can ever be. The Jewish historian Josephus and the pagan historian Tacitus both agree that Jesus was executed by order of the Roman governor of Judea. And it is very hard to imagine that Jesus' first followers would have invented such a story unless it had indeed happened. While the brute *fact* of Jesus' death by crucifixion is historically certain, however, those detailed *narratives* in our present gospels are much more problematic. They are far, far less historically certain. One other preliminary point. To look without flinching at crucifixion is painful, not only for those who have faith in Jesus, but also for those who simply have faith in humanity. Crucifixion was a cruel instrument of state terror.

Let me begin by describing crucifixion as practiced in the ancient world. One contemporary scholar has summarized the evidence as follows (Martin Hengel, *Crucifixion*, 86–88). I cite it here to invite your reading of the entire book as a detailed catalog of horror.

Crucifixion as a penalty was remarkably widespread in antiquity. It appears in various forms among numerous peoples of the ancient world, even among the Greeks. . . . [It] was and remained a political and military punishment. While among the Persians and the Carthaginians it was imposed primarily on high officials and commanders, as on rebels, among the Romans it was inflicted above all on the lower classes, i.e., slaves, violent criminals, and the unruly elements in rebellious provinces, not least in Judea. The chief reason for its use was its allegedly supreme efficacy as a deterrent; it was, of course, carried out publicly. . . . It was usually associated with other forms of torture, including at least flogging. . . . By the public display of a naked victim at a prominent place—at a crossroads, in the theater, on high ground, at the place of his crime—crucifixion also represented his uttermost humiliation. . . . Crucifixion was aggravated further by the fact that quite often its victims were never buried. It was a stereotyped picture that the crucified victim served as food for wild beasts and birds of prey. In this way his humiliation was made complete. What it meant for a man in antiquity to be refused burial, and the dishonour which went with it, can hardly be appreciated by modern man.

Notice those words about the lack of burial in cases of crucifixion. Not to allow burial attempted utterly to annihilate the human being.

I heard some time ago about the discovery of a first-century crucified skeleton. Is that correct?

In June of 1968 the only skeleton of a crucified person ever uncovered in the Jewish homeland was found in Jerusalem in a tomb that dates from the first century. It was found among the bones of thirty-five individuals whose deaths, by the way, offer a glimpse of the harshness of first-century life. Ten of those thirty-five individuals had died tragically. A woman and her infant had died together in childbirth; three children had died of starvation; five people had met violent deaths—two by burning, one by a blow from a mace-like weapon, a child by an arrow wound, and a male in his twenties by crucifixion. The name of the crucified man was Yehochanan. His arms had not been nailed, but tied, to the bar of the cross, probably with his arms to the elbows hung over and behind it. His legs had been placed on either side of the upright beam, with nails holding his heel bones to the wood on either side. There was no evidence that the man's legs had been broken, which was sometimes done in crucifixions, causing a speedier death by asphyxiation because the chest would cave in.

Crucifixion, as we have seen, was widely used in the ancient world and, by the Romans especially, inflicted on unruly elements in rebellious provinces like Judea. We know, for example, that the Syrian governor, Varus, needed three legions as well as auxiliary troops to put down revolts in the Jewish homeland, including three major messianic uprisings after the death of Herod the Great and around the time of Jesus' birth. According to Josephus, when Varus arrived in Jerusalem, he crucified two thousand rebels. Josephus also tells us that in the year 66, at the start of the first Roman-Jewish War, the Roman governor Florus had about thirty-six hundred Jewish children, women, and men scourged and crucified in a single day. Four years later, when Titus's army circled Jerusalem, many who had fled the city in search of food were caught, tortured, and crucified—according to Josephus, five hundred or more every day. My reason for listing examples of the widespread horror of crucifixion is to raise the obvious question: Why, with so many thousands crucified in the first century around Jerusalem, has only a single skeleton been found?

The reason is clear, and it is terrible to contemplate. The

three supreme Roman penalties were crucifixion, burning, and death by wild beasts. What made them supreme was not just their inhuman cruelty or their public dishonor, but the fact that there might be nothing left of a person to bury at the end. The bodily destruction in being cast into the fire or thrown to the beasts is obvious enough, but what we often don't realize about crucifixion is the carrion crow who croaks above the cross and the scavenger dogs who growl beneath the dead or dying bodies. Greco-Roman authors who wrote on the subject mentioned the crucified ones as "evil food for birds of prey and grim pickings for dogs." That was the harsh reality of crucifixion in the first century.

But what on earth did Jesus do to end up crucified—particularly if that was reserved for rebels—since he avoided open resistance to Roman rule?

That's a difficult question, and it will take some time for us to sort out.

We begin with the tradition of the gospels that say Jesus was crucified around the time of Passover. Although the gospel writers disagree on the precise timing, I see no reason not to accept as historical the general connection of Jesus' death with the Passover festival.

Remember what Passover was about. It was a celebration of the deliverance of the Jews from slavery in Egypt and their liberation as they moved toward the Promised Land. Obviously, that was a festival with very dangerous overtones in a colonized country under foreign yoke. It wouldn't have taken much imagination for first-century Jews to identify contemporary Romans with the ancient Egyptians from whose domination they had been set free. We know that huge crowds came together in a very concentrated space in Jerusalem. When Josephus wrote about an earlier Passover celebration after the death of Herod the

Great, he mentioned "an innumerable multitude of people [who] come down from the country and even from abroad to worship God." That particular phrase appears in the context of an episode in which the assembled crowds resisted the troops of Archelaus, one of Herod's heirs, who thereupon attacked them with the result that about three thousand worshipers were slaughtered in the Temple precincts. That incident demonstrates how explosive a situation Passover could be: Crowds gathered amid present oppression to celebrate deliverance from ancient oppression. At Passover time Pilate brought extra troops from Caesarea to the Antonia fortress overlooking the Temple courts. He was fully prepared to stop any trouble before it could even begin, and this explosive situation is the historical context of Jesus' arrest and death.

But that still doesn't answer the question of what Jesus did to get himself arrested and crucified.

Let us look at two separate incidents from the days immediately before Jesus' arrest, to see which might best explain what happened to him.

First, there is the story of what we usually call the "triumphal entry into Jerusalem" on what is now celebrated as Palm Sunday.

> *And they brought the colt to Jesus, and threw their garments on it; and he sat upon it. And many spread their garments on the road, and others spread leafy branches which they had cut from the fields. And those who went before and those who followed cried out, "Hosanna! Blessed is he who comes in the name of the Lord! Blessed is the kingdom of our father David that is coming! Hosanna in the highest." (Mark 11:7–10)*

Implicitly in Mark, and explicitly in Matthew and John, that action of Jesus is seen to be a fulfillment of a prophecy in Zachariah 9:9:

Lo, your king comes to you;
triumphant and victorious is he,
humble and riding on an ass,
on a colt the foal of an ass.

Certainly such a symbolic action born of messianic hopes could have provoked a repressive response from the authorities who, I have mentioned, were on heightened alert at Passover time. But the fact that it so specifically fulfills a prophetic passage makes me suspicious of its historical validity. As we have often seen, later Christian scribes looked backward to cull from the Hebrew scriptures passages that might interpret the ministry of Jesus—and sometimes those passages become the inspiration for actually creating events. So I personally doubt that the entry into Jerusalem ever actually happened.

A much more likely reason for Jesus' arrest is found in the story of the *Temple disturbance*. Here we are on much more solid historical ground; indeed, we have three independent sources for this incident.

Here is Mark's version (11:15–19) of the Temple disturbance:

And they came to Jerusalem. And he entered the temple and began to drive out those who sold and those who bought in the temple, and he overturned the tables of the money-changers and the seats of those who sold pigeons; and he would not allow any one to carry anything through the temple.
And he taught, and said to them, "Is it not written, 'My house shall be called a house of prayer for all the nations' [Isaiah 56:7]? But you have made it a den of robbers [Jeremiah 7:11]."

As I look at this story in comparison with other versions (for example in John, and the *Gospel of Thomas*), I conclude that Mark described the action of Jesus in the Temple but added to it his own scripture references (from Isaiah and Jeremiah) by way of interpretation. A version in the *Gospel of Thomas* contains a saying that more likely came from the historical Jesus. Jesus said, "I shall [destroy this] house and no one will be able to build it." That is, *Jesus was symbolically destroying the Temple*.

This trip was probably the only one Jesus ever took to Jerusalem. His vision of open table and free healing clashed wildly with what he saw in the Temple, the seat and symbol of everything that was patronal, hierarchical, brokered, even oppressive on both the religious and political level. The Temple was in the hands of high priests who were not of legitimate lineage according to Jewish law, but were hired and fired like servants by the Romans and Herodians, whose puppets they had become. Jesus' symbolic act of destruction reinforced what he had been teaching, what he had expressed through his healings, what he had effected in his practice of open eating and drinking. It was like going into a draft office during the Vietnam War and pouring blood over drawers of file cards, or like climbing a fence at a missile site and hammering on the nosecone of an ICBM. It was a symbolic negation of everything the institution stood for. No doubt Jesus' activities in Galilee might have led to his arrest at any time. But especially in the tinderbox atmosphere of the Temple at Passover time, with Pilate's forces keeping close watch, Jesus' challenge was sufficient to cause the soldiers to move in to arrest him.

Let me emphasize two points. Jesus was not "cleansing" the Temple; nor was his action some Christianity *versus* Judaism scenario. The Temple was and had to be the seat of collaboration with the Roman occupation authority. The High Priest had to be, whether he liked it or not, the link between his colonized people and their imperial overlords.

In such a situation, any Jew—even, or especially, an absolutely fervent Essene or an absolutely observant Pharisee—could have performed an action like that of Jesus. It was a symbolic destruction of the Temple as hopelessly and irrevocably contaminated and compromised. Was it the house of prayer and sacrifice or the seat of collaboration and oppression? Was the High Priest legitimate or even valid and what did such invalidity do to the house of God?

You refer to the phrase in the creed about Jesus being "crucified under Pontius Pilate," and you mention his soldiers moving in to arrest Jesus. But didn't Pilate actually try to wash his hands of the whole affair?

In the New Testament accounts, as you suggested, Pilate is portrayed as being completely just and fair, desiring to acquit Jesus but forced reluctantly and against his will to crucify him because of the insistence of Jewish authorities and the Jerusalem crowd. But what we have learned about Pontius Pilate from other records is totally at variance with that benign picture. We know quite a bit about the historical Pilate. We have archaeological as well as literary evidence for Pilate. In 1961 in the amphitheater at Caesarea a dedicatory stone to the Emperor Tiberius was found bearing the inscription "Pontius Pilate, prefect of Judea." He governed for ten years in Judea, from the years 26 to 36—a lengthy period for a second-level Roman administrator. And Josephus has told us a number of stories about Pilate's rule.

He tells us, for example, that when Pilate brought his army from Caesarea to Jerusalem for winter quarters, under cover of darkness he introduced into the city embossed medallions of the emperor attached to the military standards. This incensed the Jews, for whom the making of images was forbidden. Outraged ordinary citizens of Jerusalem walked to Caesarea and begged Pilate to remove the offending emblems. When he refused, they engaged in a sit-down strike for five days and nights around his palace. Pilate summoned the demonstrators to a stadium for an audience where he surrounded them with soldiers and threatened to kill them all unless they went home. But when the whole crowd offered their necks to the sword rather than compromise their faith, it was Pilate himself who was forced to yield rather than risk a massacre that might get unwelcome attention in Rome.

On another occasion Pilate provoked an uproar by confiscating money from the sacred treasure of the Temple in order to construct an aqueduct. This time he was smarter; he infiltrated an angry crowd with disguised soldiers in civilian dress with orders not to use their swords, but to beat the rioters with cudgels. So much for Pilate's gentle methods of crowd control.

In another incident Pilate had to deal not with massed protesters, but apocalyptic prophets. A group of Samaritans gathered at the sacred Mount Gerizim, apparently expecting an apocalyptic demonstration of God's power. Pilate suppressed the movement with a heavy hand, killing some, scattering others, and putting to death a number of leaders and prisoners. In fact, his methods were so harsh that the Syrian legate Vitellius sent Pilate off to Rome to explain himself. Even by Roman standards, therefore, Pilate was judged to be excessively cruel and unnecessarily brutal. So it is impossible for me to take as historically accurate a New Testament portrayal of Pilate as a reluctant, innocent bystander in a tragedy not of his making.

But didn't he offer to release Jesus—but the people asked for Barabbas instead?

I regard that narrative as absolutely unhistorical. First, the picture of Pilate meekly acquiescing to a shouting crowd is exactly the opposite of what we know about him from both the Jewish historian Josephus, just mentioned, and also from the contemporary Jewish philosopher, Philo of Alexandria, who used him as the model of a bad governor. Brutal crowd control was his specialty. Second, we have no evidence of a custom of open amnesty, namely, the releasing of any requested prisoner at the time of the Passover festival. The Barabbas incident did not actually happen. But I think we can readily understand why Mark created such a story.

We have talked about various kinds of resisters in the Jewish homeland: protesters, apocalyptic prophets, messianic claimants. There was one other group of peasant resisters in the first-century Jewish homeland—*rebel bandits*. Who were they? They were peasants forced off their farms who took to the hills and banditry rather than to the roads and beggary. They were not ordinary, but *social bandits*—whom other peasants might well have regarded as freedom fighters. Where you find rebel bandits you can be sure that the oppressed lower classes are being pushed below even subsistence level and forced into armed resistance, however ineffective or desperate.

There is a precise word in Greek for such a rebel bandit and that is exactly what Barabbas is called in Mark's story. He is a rebel, an insurgent, a freedom fighter. Mark wrote soon after the end of the first Roman-Jewish War when Jerusalem and its Temple had been totally destroyed in the year 70. In this story, he expressed symbolically his interpretation of that catastrophe. Among those who had carried on the futile struggle against Rome were Zealots, a loose coalition of bandit groups and peasant rebels. What Mark is saying in this story is: such was Jerusalem's choice, Barabbas over Jesus, an armed rebel over an unarmed savior. The Barabbas story was a symbolic dramatization of

Jerusalem's fate as *Mark saw it*. It tells us nothing about Jesus' trial, but it tells us much about Mark's theological perspective on the (much later) fall of Jerusalem.

But don't we have a very careful historical record of Jesus' last week? After all, we have almost an hour-by-hour account there of his trials and the events of the crucifixion.

As I mentioned at the start of this chapter, part of the difficulty in dealing with the events around the crucifixion is that the fact of the crucifixion is historically certain, but the *narratives* are very problematic. And the reason is clear. Remember how searching the scriptures created the infancy narratives that we found in Matthew and Luke? In a similar way Christian imagination took the fact of Jesus' crucifixion and fleshed it out by searching the scriptures to provide not only a rationale for his fate, but specific narratives telling its story.

Are you saying that we can't trust the gospel writers—that they are just making up stories as they go along?

I'm not suggesting that they're writing fiction in a modern sense. They were engaged in a style of religious reflection that was common to Judaism in the first century. For instance, we have all heard of the Dead Sea Scrolls. Those Scrolls, discovered in 1947, tell us about the community life of a first-century Jewish sect whose home at Qumran was destroyed during the first Roman-Jewish War. They began as a priest-led group who withdrew from Jerusalem's Temple and fled to the wilderness, believing that the Temple had been polluted by false leadership. From their long-lost library we have learned a great deal about their community and—this is my point in referring to them now—about their way of interpreting Scripture.

As the Qumran scribes applied the Hebrew Bible to their present situation, they interwove the ancient texts with their contemporary interpretations so densely that it is hard for us to tell when Bible leaves off and commentary begins. Trying to follow their interpretive work is enough to make your head spin. I won't go into too much detail, but I do want you to understand that the texts and the history could begin to interweave and to mutually influence one another. I am suggesting that a similar process occurred among some of Jesus' followers.

Two examples. The story of soldiers casting lots for Jesus' garments (see Mark 15:24) was developed from a Psalm that was often used by Christians to interpret Jesus' death:

They divide my clothes among themselves,
and for my clothing they cast lots. (Psalm 22:18)

And the story (variously told) of the suffering Jesus being given gall or poison for food, and vinegar or soured wine for drink (see Matthew 27:34) comes from another Psalm:

They gave me poison for food,
and for my thirst they gave me vinegar to drink.
(Psalm 69:21)

In the same way, other details of the crucifixion story— for instance, the spitting on and mocking of Jesus, the crown of thorns, the two thieves crucified with him, darkness at noon—all were created out of Old Testament texts.

Traditionally, Christians have said, "See how Christ's passion was foretold by the prophets." Actually, it was the other way around. The Hebrew prophets did not predict the events of Jesus' last week; rather, many of those Christian stories were created to fit the ancient prophecies in order to show that Jesus, despite his execution, was still and always held in the hands of God.

My proposal is this: Jesus' first followers knew almost nothing whatsoever about the details of his crucifixion, death, or burial. We have those detailed accounts of his final days and hours because *Old Testament texts were turned into first-century events*. That is, the Hebrew scriptures were not *predictions* of what would happen to Jesus, but were used later to *create* the stories about what happened to him; they were sought out *backwards*, as it were, after that death had occurred. Prophecy, in other words, is known after the fact rather than before it.

Recently I read an article about you in the **Detroit Free Press.** *The headline ran: "A Controversial Scholar Says Key Biblical Scenes Are Fiction that Led to Persecution of Jews." Comment?*

Nowhere is background more necessary than here. The gospels do not claim to be exact *histories* or straightforward *biographies* but *gospels*, that is, good news. Gospels must be two things: good and news. The word "good" underlines that it is from somebody's point of view, that of, say, the Christian followers of Jesus rather than the Roman authorities. The word "news" underlines the hallmark of a gospel: updating. Each gospel must not only tell the story of Jesus, it must update it for its own time and place, situation and audience. Maybe we do not like that and would prefer journalism. But whether we like it or not, gospels update. That is, of course, why we can have one Jesus but several gospels. Gospels update the words and deeds of Jesus by adopting and adapting, inventing sayings and events, debates and dialogues. So far, so good. But they also update stories of the *enemies* of Jesus, and that is where the trouble starts.

It is not as if the early Christians sat down and said, "Let

us invent lies about our enemies." Christians were originally one Jewish group among many other Jewish groups in
the first century. We should hear the word "Christians" the
way we hear words like "Pharisees," "Sadducees,"
"Essenes," "Zealots," or any other group within Judaism
at that time. They may all have been struggling for power
and control, for the hearts and minds, the destiny and leadership of their own people. But it was all within, not
against, Judaism itself. No matter what names were called
or accusations made, one could hardly talk of anti-Judaism
or anti-Semitism at that stage.

But, especially after the disaster of the first Roman-
Jewish War, Christians were becoming more and more
marginalized as a force within Judaism and were becoming
less and less likely to attain the leadership of their own people. The future would lie with Rabbinic Judaism and not
with Christian Judaism.

As described by Mark in the 70s, Jesus' enemies at the
crucifixion are "the crowd" from Jerusalem. By Matthew in
the 80s, that crowd has grown to "all the people." And by
John in the 90s, it has become, quite simply, "the Jews." I
do not think that even John means the Jews as distinct from
non-Jews. He means: all those other bad Jews except us
good Jews! It is as if some Americans were to say,
"Americans are too violent," not thereby denying that they
were themselves American but meaning: all those bad
Americans except us good Americans.

None of that process, even in its nastiest name-calling,
made much difference in the second or third centuries
when Christianity, though by then a religion distinct from
Judaism, had no power of reprisal. But in the fourth century, when the Roman Empire became officially Christian,
those very same crucifixion stories took on the meaning of
Christians accusing Jews, and began the long and lethal
process that prepared Europe for the Holocaust in the
terrible fullness of time.

My point in *Who Killed Jesus?* was that we must understand those crucifixion accounts and calculate especially the
updating process intrinsic to gospel. We must also, as contemporary Christians, discuss responsibly what to do with
the public reading and private study of those texts, lest the
anti-Semitic hate they have fueled in the past continue to
haunt the future. That was why the book's subtitle read:
*Exposing the Roots of Anti-Semitism in the Gospel Story of the
Death of Jesus.*

***We've talked about what didn't happen. What do you
think actually happened during those last days of Jesus'
life?***

My best historical reconstruction would be something
like this. Jesus was arrested during the Passover festival,
most likely in response to his action in the Temple. Those
who were closest to him ran away for their own safety. I do
not presume that there were any high-level confrontations
between Caiaphas and Pilate and Herod Antipas either
about Jesus or with Jesus. No doubt they would have
agreed before the festival that fast action was to be taken
against any disturbance and that a few examples by crucifixion might be especially useful at the outset. And I doubt
very much if Jewish police or Roman soldiers needed to go
too far up the chain of command in handling a Galilean
peasant like Jesus. It is hard for us to imagine the casual
brutality with which Jesus was probably taken and executed. All those "last week" details in our gospels, as distinct
from the brute facts just mentioned, are prophecy turned
into history, rather than history remembered.

***You mentioned earlier that it was customary for crucified
bodies to be left for the beasts. But in Jesus' case, wasn't he
buried in a tomb owned by Joseph of Arimathea?***

First of all, it was *possible* for a crucified body to be given back to its family for burial. That certainly was the case with the Yehochanan whom I mentioned at the beginning of this chapter. But it was very unusual. In a patronal society, getting permission for such a burial would have taken some influence. In general, if you had influence, you did not end up crucified, and if you ended up crucified, you would not have enough influence to be buried. Normally soldiers guarded the body until death, and thereafter it was left for carrion crow, scavenger dog, or other wild beast to finish the brutal job. And as I said earlier, the horror of nonburial was part of the crucifixion routine, intended by the authorities to serve as a dreadful warning to every passerby.

Of course, we cannot know with certainty what happened to the body of Jesus, but we can see clearly how much concern there was in the developing Christian tradition about the disposition of his body. The accounts steadily become more dignified and elaborate, as the horror of the brutal truth was, through hope and imagination, turned into appropriate and even regal burial.

To begin with, in the *Gospel of Peter*, a text not found in the New Testament, we are simply told that the dead Jesus was buried by those who had crucified him. That story grows out of the Jewish terror of nonburial, expressed in Deuteronomy 21:22–23:

> *When someone is convicted of a crime punishable by death and is executed, and you hang him on a tree, his corpse must not remain all night upon the tree; you shall bury him that same day, for anyone hung on a tree is under God's curse.*

Christians *hoped* that those who crucified Jesus might have buried him in deference to that ancient text. But as the tradition grew, Jesus' burial was moved from enemies to friends, from inadequate and hurried to full and complete.

That brings us to the well-known story in Mark 15:42–46:

When evening had come, and since it was the day of Preparation, that is, the day before the sabbath, Joseph of Arimathea, a respected member of the council, who was also himself waiting expectantly for the kingdom of God, went boldly to Pilate and asked for the body of Jesus. Then Pilate wondered if he were already dead; and summoning the centurion, he asked him whether he had been dead for some time. When he learned from the centurion that he was dead, he granted the body to Joseph. Then Joseph bought a linen cloth, and taking down the body, wrapped it in the cloth, and laid it in a tomb that had been hewn out of the rock. He then rolled a stone against the door of the tomb.

I regard this story as the creation of Mark. (By the way, the naming of Joseph of Arimathea, as in the case of Barabbas, does not necessarily guarantee historical accuracy. If you are inventing a person, it is easy to invent a name for him as well.) Notice what Mark has done. Joseph is both "a respected member of the council"—that is, on the side of those who crucified Jesus—and also "waiting expectantly for the kingdom of God"—that is, on the side of Jesus and his followers. Matthew and Luke each try to improve on the story. Matthew describes Joseph as "a disciple of Jesus"—rather than as a member of the council that condemned Jesus. Luke keeps Joseph on the council but says that "though a member of the council, he had not agreed to their plan and action." Both Matthew and Luke are trying to solve the problem in Mark's story; namely, how is it that Joseph was both part of the council that condemned Jesus and the one who sought his body for respectful burial? Finally, when John tells the story, he combines Joseph of Arimathea with the Nicodemus who had shown up earlier in his gospel, and has them giving Jesus what we may only term a royal burial in a brand new tomb located in the midst of a garden. And now Joseph is described as a disciple of Jesus, "though a secret one because of his fear of the Jews."

As I watch the development of the burial story, I find it impossible to avoid the conclusion that we have here an intense and understandable effort to avoid the stark horror of crucifixion's final act. The worst possible horror was no burial at all, Jesus left on the cross for the scavengers. The next best hope was burial by his enemies. But it was better not to imagine how soldiers might have done that: with lime? in a shallow grave? under a pile of stones? The next best possibility was some authority figure deciding to bury Jesus. But that would create credibility problems and besides, unless Jesus was in a separate grave all to himself, you could not have a story about finding an empty tomb! Best of all would be to have Jesus buried by those who loved him.

But is it possible *that he was buried?*

Yes, it is possible. What I must deal with, as a historian, is *probability*. If I were giving testimony in a courtroom, and I were asked in cross-examination, "Now, Professor Crossan, isn't it *possible* that . . ." I would have to answer, "Yes—of course." In historical reconstruction we do not deal in certainties. What I have offered here—and elsewhere—is my best judgment, based on my historical research—of the most likely scenario.

As you've retold the story of Jesus' arrest and execution, it sounds very human—he challenges the powers that be in the name of a new social vision, and they crush him. But how do you get from that to a theology claiming Jesus died to save us from our sins?

I think it helps to distinguish between three ways of looking at it—*history*, *faith*, and *theology*. The *history* is clear: Jesus died by crucifixion under the Roman governor, Pontius Pilate. People who had *faith* in Jesus found meaning in that execution—he died for *us*. A developing *theology* worked out the idea that his death made atonement for human sin. Let's take a look at each of these ideas.

The crucifixion of Jesus was a terrible shock to the hopes of those who had followed him. A shameful death was not the fate they expected for someone with whom, in open table and shared healing, they had experienced the dawning of the Kingdom of God. So they had to try to make sense of it.

Faith found meaning in the *history*. We can certainly imagine a Hindu "untouchable" in India in our own century saying of the assassinated Gandhi, "He died for me." A black garbage collector in Memphis might have said of Martin Luther King, Jr., "He died for me." Both would be speaking in a historically realistic way, for in seeking the well-being of these oppressed, marginalized groups, Gandhi and King made their own deaths almost inevitable. It is not hard to imagine a Galilean peasant, aware that Jesus' vision brought him into conflict with powerful forces, saying, "He died for me."

And they would naturally express that faith in language of their own religious tradition. Soon after Jesus' death, as we have noted before, his more learned followers began to search their scriptures for clues to its meaning. In Leviticus 16 they found a ritual for atonement, in which the High Priest would confess the people's sins over a goat, which would be sent out into the wilderness, symbolically carrying those sins away. To some Christians, that came to be a prophecy about Jesus, who bore the people's sins. Of course, that is a meaningful image only to people in a religious tradition that emphasizes *blood sacrifice*.

In other Christian communities—like the one from

which we get the *Q Gospel*—such sacrificial theology had no influence. The Q community regarded Jesus as the Wisdom of God. They would have talked of his death like this: Wisdom, which comes from God, is always persecuted and destroyed—but will return. *Their* theology would be: the world's powers destroyed Jesus, but he has returned to God, and he is with us *despite his death*, as God's Wisdom. They could speak of the meaning of Jesus' death without any sacrificial metaphors at all.

What about *our* way of speaking? My problem is this: language of blood sacrifice was appropriate to people used to the sacrifices that were part of ancient temple worship, but is totally alien to our world. In our society, if anyone tried blood sacrifice of even cows or sheep or goats, we would quickly make it illegal. Moreover, an atonement theology that says God sacrificed his own son in place of humans who needed to be punished for their sins might make some Christians love Jesus, but is an obscene picture of God. It is almost heavenly child abuse, and may infect our imagination at more earthly levels as well. I do not want to express my faith through a theology that pictures God demanding blood sacrifices in order to be reconciled to us.

But the last supper and the Christian Eucharist celebrate the death of Jesus. How does that fit with all you have said?

During his life Jesus enacted the Kingdom's presence by celebrating an open table—but it was a real meal for real people and most often for those who otherwise would not have eaten at all. We might sneer and call that a pot-luck Kingdom, since we eat regularly and share, when we share, our plenty with each other. For many of the first Christians, that open table meant all the food they were sure of having. And God, they believed, was their host. But Jesus died for that vision and because of that program. Inevitably and rightly, then, that open table came both to celebrate his life and commemorate his death.

You have not mentioned anything about Peter's denial. Is that event symbolic or historical?

That story derives from Mark and is copied from him into Matthew, Luke, and John. It is told with a stylistic device characteristic of Mark, in which a second incident is sandwiched between the start and finish of a first one and the two are intended to vibrate together interpretatively. For example, Jesus curses the fig tree, Jesus "destroys" the Temple, Jesus finds the fig tree withered in Mark 11:12–20. Cursed fig tree and destroyed Temple interpret one another for Mark. So also here, Jesus' courageous confession under trial is sandwiched between the start and finish of Peter's cowardly denials. But, of course, Peter is forgiven at the end. That sandwich is a Markan creation directed to his own community, during or after the Jewish War against Rome of 66–74. Mark's community knew all about persecution from both the Roman and the Jewish side, and this is his own consoling story: Be brave like Jesus, but even if you betray like Peter, you may still expect forgiveness. I presume that Peter ran away as did most of Jesus' companions (losing their nerve but not their faith) and this story uses him, because of his leadership status, as a model for denial forgiven. The story of Peter's denial is symbolical rather than historical.

Does the same apply to Judas' betrayal? Is that historical or not?

That is a much more difficult and delicate problem. It

has been suggested that Judas-as-traitor was deliberately created as an anti-Semitic slur, since the name "Judas" means "the Jew." Such a reading could easily have arisen among pagan Christians but hardly among Jewish Christians. Jesus, for example, has a brother named Judas or Jude. Fellow Jews would hardly hear "Judas" as "the Jew" in distinction from those who were not Jews. So unless the Judas story was created rather late and in a pagan Christian environment, I cannot accept that argument. Furthermore, unlike the case of Peter's denials, (derived exclusively from Mark), Judas's betrayal is found in several other independent sources, for example, Matthew 27:3–10 and Acts 1:18–20. The role of this betrayer was probably not just to locate Jesus at night, when he could be arrested quietly, since the authorities were quite ready for a public execution. The betrayal may have involved identification and not just location. Suppose, as a pure guess, that the authorities had grabbed one of Jesus' companions after the Temple incident and needed to know who had caused the trouble. That is the sort of role I imagine for Judas. Jesus was crucified in Judea and it is not anti-Semitic to say that. Jesus was betrayed by Judas and neither is it anti-Semitic to say that. I do not think, by the way, that Judas was ever one of the Twelve Apostles. The Twelve were created only after the death of Jesus, when Peter led the mission for Jewish converts and the Twelve Apostles represented that new Israel, just as the twelve patriarchs had represented the older Israel.

8

What Happened on Easter Sunday?

*Y*our *book cleans up "the story" for me; an accomplishment basic in any effort to restore the presentation of the Christian faith to a level of credibility vital to its survival as a major moral force in the world. . . . And, in our enlightenment, bonfires need not, must not, be put to the contrived stories of Jesus' descent from David, or the Virgin Birth, the Resurrection. . . . Let us keep and cherish them as the lovely myths that they are, the attesting poetry of the zealous, but let us be honest and simply recognize them for what they are, and know and accept them as such. . . . What the church should be and teach is far too important to be buried and obscured behind the centuries-accumulated wall of its careless and considered droppings.*

A person from Vermont

I want to thank you for your two books on the historical Jesus. I have waited for these books ever since I was ten or twelve years old. [Writer is at least eighty-five years old at this time]. . . . You will be interested to know that there are some alert church members who are showing an interest in what you have written and who want to make a serious study of the historical Jesus.

A man from Iowa

The historical Jesus you described provided a new way for our church to think of Him that, if needed, enhances his stature in modern terms. . . . You have stimulated my religious curiosity

and sober investigation and I know stimulated others. . . .
                                                    A man from Illinois

I have to write you this letter thanking you for works in recent years concerning the "historical Jesus.". . . As a Christian not willing to have a lobotomy, I find your honesty concerning what we really know about Jesus very refreshing. In an age when fundamentalists and their threats have cowed so many scholars from seeking the truth, your works stand out. . . . In fact, I would say that my faith has actually been strengthened by knowing and understanding the context in which Jesus lived and worked.
                                                    A man from Illinois

While a student in the 70s I was affiliated with the Catholic Worker movement, which emphasized the radical aspect of the teachings of Jesus. This experience inspired me to a career in geriatrics. I find that the dying are not comforted by the historical Jesus, they are more comforted by the good news proclaimed in its entirety followed by: "This is the word of the Lord." This includes the message . . . that proclaims an "empty tomb" and appearances to women, and Thomas, who was told to physically examine the wounds. If it is not true, then Christianity is a two-thousand-year hoax and fraud. As Paul states: Christians are the most miserable of the miserable if this complete message is poisoned by mythology.
                                                    A woman from Florida

I liked your book [Jesus: A Revolutionary Biography] *and hope it will contribute to the long-range effect of putting Jesus' message in a more rational framework. It seems to me that your point of view may strengthen the message rather than weaken it—although I must say that over the years (I was raised a Methodist) I have found the whole idea of Jesus' resurrection, at least in the traditional sense, and the concept of a "life after death," that is, the idea that my consciousness will somehow survive my death, increasingly difficult to accept—even though I remain interested in religion and fond of my memories of church.*
                                                    A man from Michigan

Works like yours that discredit Jesus bring accolades and high praise from a secular world but man does not have the last word. I am not a priest or a pastor but a Christian who cannot stand by while such attacks are being waged without speaking up. Remember, Jesus had to knock Saul off his mule and temporarily blind him in order to get his attention. Therefore, I challenge and invite you, in Christian love, to humble yourself and seek Him, then and only then will He make Himself known to you as He did me and you won't have to question His divinity or His resurrection—you will know—He is risen!!

A man from West Virginia

The statement [attributed to Dr. Crossan in the Chicago Tribune Magazine *of July 17, 1994 by Jeff Lyon] about Jesus not resurrecting from the dead is absurd. Are you trying to say that after his execution He did not rise from the dead? In other words you think that he is still dead. Well, as far as I'm concerned, my Jesus is alive because he lives inside my heart. I can also see his wonders every day. He keeps me alive by the air I breathe. He protects me, feeds me, clothes me, and supplies my needs. So how dare you say He never resurrected from the dead. Even the Bible says so.*

A girl from Illinois

What about Easter Sunday?

In discussing the crucifixion, I argued that the story of Jesus' burial by his friends was totally unhistorical. If he was buried at all, he was buried not by his friends but by his enemies. And not in a tomb hewed out of stone, but in a shallow grave that would have made his body easy prey for scavenging animals. Those are grim conclusions, but I cannot escape them.

With the Easter stories, are we standing on the solid rock of historical fact? Or, if not, how are we to account for the survival of faith in Jesus? And if we decide that we cannot read the Easter narratives literally, then how *are* we to read them? I raise these questions not just because for some twentieth-century people the notion of resurrection from the dead seems incredible on the face of it. I raise these questions also because the New Testament record forces me to raise them. Matthew, Mark, Luke, and John tell the Easter story quite differently—so differently, in fact, that we simply cannot harmonize their versions. So we have to ask questions of intention and meaning.

In a nutshell, these are my conclusions: First, the Easter story is not about the events of a single day, but reflects the struggle of Jesus' followers over a period of months and years to make sense of both his death and their continuing experience of empowerment by him. Second, stories of the resurrected Jesus appearing to various people are not really about "visions" at all, but are literary fiction prompted by struggles over leadership in the early Church. Third, resurrection is one—but only one—of the metaphors used to express the sense of Jesus' continuing presence with his followers and friends.

So you're saying that the Easter story is just a fairy tale— a sort of Hollywood happy ending

No, I'm not saying that at all. But you could certainly get that impression if you just read the accounts in the gospels uncritically. You know how the story goes: Friday was tragic, Saturday was desolate, on Sunday the tomb was empty and all was well.

It's perfectly true that Jesus' followers fled when he was taken and executed. And that's entirely understandable. But it's a terrible trivialization to suppose that they all lost their faith on Friday and miraculously got it back on Sunday. I have tremendous respect for those first Christians. I think that, far from losing their faith when Jesus was killed, they kept it alive and even deepened it.

But what about the empty tomb?

Is the story of the empty tomb historical? No. I've already explained why I doubt there was any tomb for Jesus in the first place. I don't think any of Jesus' followers even knew where he was buried—if he was buried at all. And the gospel writers don't come close to agreeing with each other on what they report. So my conviction is that motives other than just history writing are clearly at work here.

By the way, Paul is the earliest writer we have on resurrection—his letters are much earlier than the gospels—and he nowhere shows awareness of having heard an empty tomb story. That's hard to understand, if an empty tomb was supposed to be the bedrock historical fact of Easter.

Well, what are the bedrock historical facts, then?

Let's look for a moment completely outside the records produced by Christians. Are there any "outside" witnesses we can call upon for some help? The answer is yes.

First, there is the Jewish historian I've often referred to, Josephus. Writing near the end of the first century, he describes Jesus as a wise man "who wrought surprising feats," was accused by high-standing Jewish leaders, and put to death by Pilate. But, Josephus adds, "those who had in the first place come to love him did not give up their affection for him," so that "the tribe of the Christians, so called after him, has still to this day not disappeared."

The second witness is the Roman historian Tacitus, writing early in the second century. He mentions that

"Christus" had been sentenced to death by the procurator Pontius Pilate. Then, with a sneer, he notes that the "pernicious superstition" of his followers, far from being snuffed out, even found its way to Rome, "where all things horrible or shameful in the world collect and find a vogue."

So we have two outside sources, one neutral in tone and one insulting. But both agree on the outline of what happened. There was a movement over there in the "colony." Its founder was executed by Pilate. But, instead of ending there, as might have been expected, the movement continued, and has now reached Rome itself. Tacitus and Josephus, of course, are not Christians, and don't speak of "resurrection." But they do witness to *unexpected continuity* in the movement connected with Jesus.

That's a long way from resurrection, though.

Perhaps. But maybe resurrection is simply a word-picture of Jesus' continuing presence among his followers.

In the *Gospel of Thomas*, for example, only one title is ever used of Jesus. He is called simply the "Living Jesus." His followers experience him as the Wisdom of God on earth, still present and acting, just as when he was walking around their countryside. Those missionaries we talked about earlier, sent out by Jesus to offer free healing and share open meals in the homes and hamlets of Galilee—do you really think they just dropped everything the day he died? Just immediately all lost their faith? No. I think that they found themselves just as empowered as they had been before. And that meant that somehow Jesus was still with them. So they struggled to find a way to express that powerful and empowering *presence* of Jesus. That way *was* the Easter story.

You talked about Easter as not one day, but a period of months or even years. What do you mean by that?

What I mean is that Jesus' execution forced his followers to wrestle with some very tough questions. How could he have come to such a fate? How could Jesus have suffered a disgraceful death at the hands of imperial authority and still be what their experience persuaded them he was—God's wisdom and power? You might picture two different groups of Christians. The itinerant missionaries in Galilee worked it out with their hot, sore feet as they walked from house to house continuing his mission. The more scholarly sorts in Jerusalem pored over the texts of their scriptures to understand what had happened. Not because they had *lost* their faith, but because they were trying to *understand* and *explain* how it was that their faith persisted in spite of what had happened.

The Emmaus Road story in Luke 24, mentioned in Chapter 6, is a good example. Think about it not as a single day that you could have caught on your camcorder if you had been there, but as a pictorial summary of the whole rethinking struggle I described above. See if it makes sense to you that way.

In the story, the two itinerant missionaries are going out on Easter Sunday from the Jerusalem community toward Emmaus, seven miles down the road. As they walk, they're deep in sorrow, talking about the terrible events of Jesus' arrest and crucifixion. A stranger joins them and asks what they're discussing. They can't believe he doesn't know what's been happening, and tell him about the execution of Jesus, who was "a prophet mighty in deed and word before God and all the people." And they report the strange tales of women who had found his tomb empty. The stranger rebukes them for being "slow of heart" in believing what the Jewish scriptures say, and asks rhetorically, "Was it not necessary that the Messiah should suffer these things and then enter into his glory?"

But Cleopas and his companion still don't understand who they're talking to. When they approach Emmaus, the stranger appears intent on going on, but they talk him into staying with them. They go in to eat. Listen to the story:

When he was at the table with them, he took bread, blessed and broke it, and gave it to them. Then their eyes were opened, and they recognized him; and he vanished from their sight. They said to each other, "Were not our hearts burning within us while he was talking to us on the road, while he was opening the scriptures to us?"

That's the story. If you ask me whether it's historical in the sense of being a straightforward account of what happened to two people on Easter Sunday, I say no. But it is *certainly* historical in the sense of describing a *process over time* that happened in the Christian community. That is, they did come to believe that the Living Jesus "opened their minds to understand the scriptures." They did find in their tradition the hints they were looking for that, despite his ignominious death, Jesus was the agent of God's purpose. And he did keep meeting them "in the breaking of the bread." That is, as Christians continued to gather for the open communal meals to which Jesus had introduced them, they experienced him as present. Continuing to empower them for the work of the Kingdom, he was the "Living Jesus."

You might put it this way: the Emmaus story isn't a fact, but it is true. It's a symbolic picture of Christian faith deepening over time. Easter was much, much more than the events of a single day.

Okay, that makes sense. But I still want to go back to the idea of resurrection. After all, that seems to be a central New Testament claim. Right?

Right. I'm saying that resurrection is only one of several ways that Christians could think about their experience of "Jesus-with-us." So the question is where that emphasis on resurrection comes from. And the answer is: from Paul.

If you look at 1 Corinthians 15, you find Paul—and this is twenty to forty years before the gospels were written—defending the idea of bodily resurrection. But here's a very interesting twist: He never argues that resurrection was a special miracle only for Jesus. Just the opposite: Jesus' resurrection is for him one instance of a *general* resurrection.

It's easy to see how he develops his argument. Before his conversion, Paul had been a devout Pharisee—and Pharisees believed that God would raise up the righteous dead at the end of "this present age." Paul, as you know, was on his way to Damascus to persecute Christians when he had an experience that we would call *vision* or *trance*—a blinding light, a voice, a fall to the ground. To Paul, this was an encounter with the Jesus he was attacking. How would he understand this experience of Jesus? I think the answer is that he would conclude that *the general resurrection has begun*. In fact, that's exactly the way he describes his belief: Jesus is "the first fruits of those who have died." Given his expectation of a general resurrection, his experience of Jesus would persuade him that it had in fact begun. Jesus isn't the *only* one to be raised, just the *first*.

It is significant that Paul does not say, "If Christ's tomb is not empty, vain is our faith," but, "if Christ is not risen, vain is our faith." He is not talking about the resuscitation of Jesus' corpse but about the presence of Jesus in a wholly new mode of existence. It is, for Paul, the same Jesus who once was an earthly presence limited by time and place, who now is a transcendant presence unlimited by time and place.

So Paul was wrong about the resurrection?

No, I'm not saying that Paul was wrong. Just that his experience was *his* experience—not everybody else's. But I don't see any reason to believe that *all* of Jesus' followers would have reasoned the same way. After all, most of them were peasants, not Pharisees like Paul with a sophisticated training in interpretation of scripture. And since Paul had been a bitter enemy of the movement, his trance-experience would have been a unique outworking of his own psychological conflict. So I don't see any reason to suppose that either his experience or the way he interpreted it (that is, as a meeting with a resurrected Jesus) was typical of other Christians. As I said before, those peasant followers in Galilee knew Jesus' presence in their sore feet. Those scribes in Jerusalem were meeting him again in their study of scripture. So Paul's use of the category of resurrection was just one possible way of talking about the presence and power of Jesus in the lives of his followers.

In fact, I'd go even further. Paul's image of Jesus as the "first fruits of those who have died" depends upon the notion that the full harvest is at hand. But if that isn't the case, the metaphor doesn't work very well. If Paul were here today, I might ask him, "Paul, we've been waiting a long time since the 'first fruits' for that harvest you talked about. Maybe you weren't quite right about that general resurrection being just around the corner. Is there a better way to talk about Jesus' presence among us than 'resurrection?'"

How do you personally think about it? What is your own Easter faith?

Easter means for me that the divine empowerment which was present in Jesus, but once upon a time limited to those people in Galilee and Judea who had contact with him, is now available to anyone, anywhere in the world, who finds God in Jesus. As far as I'm concerned, it has nothing to do, literally, with a body coming out of a tomb, or a tomb being found empty, or visions, or anything else. All those are dramatic ways of expressing the faith. The heart of resurrection for me is that the power of God is now available through Jesus, unconfined by time or space, to anyone who believes and experiences it.

But what about all the stories of the risen Jesus appearing to people? If Easter for you doesn't have anything to do with visions or a literal resurrection, what do you do with all those stories?

That's a very important question. Let me tell you what I've concluded, and then give an illustration or two.

We usually regard those stories of post-Easter appearances by Jesus as visions of some sort. I think they're nothing of the kind. They have no marks that you would expect—no blinding lights, no heavenly voices, nobody knocked to the ground. Neither does Jesus bring back from "the other side" some new revelation, as you might expect. Rather, what really matters is *who Jesus appears to*. That is, these stories are dramatizations with a political purpose. And that purpose is to tell us who's in charge, now that Jesus is no longer personally present.

Here's the clearest example. In John 20, you have a story of a race by two disciples to the empty tomb. Peter and the unnamed follower called the Beloved Disciple run toward the tomb. The Beloved Disciple outraces Peter, gets to the tomb, looks in and is the first to see the discarded linen wrappings. Because there was an older tradition that *Peter* had been the first to the tomb, he is allowed in this version to actually enter the tomb first. But when the Beloved Disciple next enters the tomb, he alone is said to *see and believe*. Thus he takes first place away from Peter.

But there's more. Next to be subordinated to the Beloved Disciple is Mary Magdalene. In Matthew's gospel (28:8–10) she meets and worships the risen Jesus. But here in John she fails to recognize Jesus when he appears to her, and three times gives the wrong interpretation of the empty tomb: "They have taken away my Lord." And finally, the Beloved Disciple is exalted over Thomas, whom we have immortalized as "Doubting Thomas." In this story he refuses to believe unless and until he can personally see and touch the wounds from the crucifixion. When Jesus does appear to him, he is rebuked in words that at the same time honor the Beloved Disciple: "Have you believed because you have seen me? Blessed are those who have not seen and yet have come to believe."

Stories like that tell us absolutely nothing of historical value about the origins of Christian faith. But they tell us a great deal about the origins of Christian *authority*. They are competing pictures about who has priority and power in the early Christian community. John 20, for example, tells us that in the community of the Beloved Disciple, Mary Magdalene's authority had to be challenged as much as that of Peter or Thomas. And, of course, we have outside the New Testament a *Gospel of Peter*, a *Gospel of Mary*, and a *Gospel of Thomas*. Stories like this presume a community that has been around for a long time—probably for one or two generations. But they really have nothing to do with appearances on Easter Sunday. They are dramatizations about where power and authority rest in the early Church.

And they're not entirely innocent stories, either. If you read them carefully, you'll find that the trend is away from Jesus' egalitarian community toward investing authority either in a leadership group (the Twelve) or in specific individuals (e.g. Peter or the Beloved Disciple). Already we're on our way toward a church led by a male hierarchy. And that's a long way from where Jesus started.

So the "appearance" stories aren't the historical record of one day—Easter Sunday—right?

That's what I'm arguing, yes. There may well have been visions, of course. There are always visions in religion, and Paul certainly had a vision of Jesus. My point is that those stories in the last chapters of the gospels are not and were not intended to describe visions.

Then summarize if you will what we are left with, historically.

What happened historically is that those who believed in Jesus before his execution *continued* to do so afterward. Easter is not about the start of a new faith but the continuation of an old one. Despite his crucifixion, Jesus was for his followers alive, present, and empowering them to do the work of the Kingdom still. That's the only mystery and the only miracle, and as far as I'm concerned, it's more than enough of both. Of course, there may have been visions and trances. There are always such in every religion, and I've no reason to think that Paul was alone in his. But the basic reality is that those whom Jesus empowered as healers and invited around an open table kept his vision and program alive, and continued to experience his presence in that vision and program. That, to me, is Easter.

Do you personally believe in life after death for us?

First, a little bit of history. In the entire Old Testament until the time of the Maccabees in the second century before Jesus, there is not the slightest hint of belief in an afterlife, even though the whole world around Israel believed it. As far as those scriptures were concerned, God was eternal but people, even God's people, were not. If they had eternal life, it was by being part of God's people because God's people as a community lived on. I've looked at Jewish grave engravings from the second and third centuries of our era, and even then the views are mixed, some with belief in afterlife, some not. So belief in life after death has certainly not always been part of biblical faith.

Second, I think we need to raise a question: Is the primary purpose of God to guarantee our immortality? It would seem to be so for many people to whom, if there is no immortality, there's no sense of even believing in God.

Third, I do think that part of our human need is to create what I call "metaphors of immortality." That is, we all need something bigger than ourselves to live for, and something bigger than ourselves to live on after us. That may be a family, a nation, an organization, a church, or whatever is authentically and communally greater than our own individuality. A metaphor of immortality gives life and death meaning.

Do I personally believe in an afterlife? No, but to be honest, I do not find it a particularly important question one way or the other. I am not in the least bit interested in fighting those who believe or hope in it. My own interest is in how we live our lives here below. I am sure that we are called to do the will of God "on earth, as in heaven." Heaven, however, I leave up to God. Earth is where our responsibility lies, that is where the Kingdom of God is lost or found.

But if we build the meaning of this present life on its being eternal, I'm pretty sure we're wrong. Or if we use the prospect of eternal life to dull us to the present world and its injustices, we're wrong. If there is not enough meaning in life that we must imagine having it in a future life, we're wrong. I think those in earlier generations who painted pictures of hell as well as heaven had it right—they saw both good and evil in the human story. Their problem was that they banished heaven and hell to the future. Our problem is that we try to believe in heaven without facing hell. My view is that both heaven and hell are present here and now. We make life. We make this world heaven or hell. So far, and in general, we have made it more hell than heaven. To put it in biblical terms: either we try to fashion the world in the image of the Kingdom Jesus envisioned, or we abandon it to the world's Caesars and Pilates.

How Do You Get from Jesus to Christ?

*Earlier tonight my friend came by with his son.
I read him a couple of lines from Crossan
having to do with forms of peasant resistance.
I do not say anything about Jesus to my friend
although he is always more than kind when I do.
In fact, I discuss Jesus more
with my Buddhist friends than I do with Christians.
This is a painful fact. Let me quote one sentence:
"Open commensality has been both ritualized,
which was probably inevitable,
and ruined, which was not."
I have not been a model of faith.
I have been nowhere all night waiting for this book.*
                                        A man from Washington

*For Dominic: You have provided a framework within which I
could say I am a Christian—something I have not been able to
say for very many years.*
                                        A person from Minnesota

*I apologize to you, for the damage I did to you during my
undergraduate studies in Christianity. . . . Without so much
as having even opened one of your books, [my classmates and I]
badgered you and then dismissed you in what we labeled your*

turpitude. . . . I received the book [Jesus: A Revolutionary Biography] *as a present but didn't read it until recently. . . . I believe that you have raised serious questions which demand the soulful attention of all religious people. . . . Your writing bears the mark of aweful, soul-empowering inspiration. You have shown me how to open some doors for myself—to have the courage to question what I know I should question. I will pray for the strength of heart that you've demonstrated in your book.*

A man from Virginia

Most United Kingdom clergy, for example, take for granted that Jesus said or did everything that is recorded in the Gospels. Our group finds it increasingly irksome having to endure sermons and lectures which ignore the most elementary conclusions of biblical scholarship. Living with the gap is challenging. On the one hand, it enables us to speak with nonchurchgoing professionals about Jesus and his followers in ways which do not insult their intelligence and integrity. On the other hand, the paradigm shift has such radical consequences for normal church discourse and worship that very few church people can face them. Do you also encounter this gap?

A group from England

You intimated somewhat through your writing that you did not believe historically, and I would venture to say personally, that Jesus was the Son of God, as is accepted in orthodox Christianity. And so I wonder what exactly your impression of modern-day Christianity is? What do you think of the millions of people who believe in a future Kingdom of God based upon the death and resurrection of Jesus, the atonement of mankind's sin through his sacrificial death, and the concept of eternal salvation as being a gift according to the grace of God, do you think that they are all misled and wrong?

A woman from California

Let's suppose your picture of the historical Jesus is right on tar-

*get. What does that mean for me as a disciple of Jesus? In con-
crete terms, what would following Jesus look like today? How
should Christians live today?*

A man from Virginia

**It's time for a summing-up. If someone who had never
heard of Jesus asks you to tell his story in just two or three
minutes, what would you say?**

I'd say that Jesus lived in an occupied land, among peasants who had long existed at a subsistence level and were
being pressed harder and harder. It was a world of structured inequality and injustice. In *that world*, he offered and
lived out an alternative vision. And he invited others to
share it: a community of free healing and shared eating, a
community of equals before God and each other. To
women, children, men, to lepers, the destitute, the dis-
turbed, he issued the same invitation: Come eat with me
and be healed, and take what you experience to others.
That new community was what the Kingdom of God
looked like, what the whole world would look like if God,
not Caesar, were directly in charge. That is what it means
for God's will to be done on earth as in heaven.

But "heaven" was in good shape—*earth* was the problem.
That's why Jesus didn't just talk about the Kingdom, but
acted it out. He plowed the vision of the Kingdom into the
soil of his own society. That made him a revolutionary figure—not in a military sense, but in a social sense. And he
died for his vision of the Kingdom. Though his sharp challenge to the usual arrangements of his world could have
gotten him arrested at any time, his symbolic destruction of
the Temple provided the immediate excuse for high Jewish
and Roman authorities to move against him. And we can
hardly even imagine the brutal offhandedness with which a
peasant nobody like Jesus would have been crushed in a

Jerusalem under the likes of Caiaphas and Pilate.

But what was totally unexpected was that the end of this troublesome Jewish peasant was not the end after all. Those who had originally experienced God's power through their life together with him continued to experience it after his death. Now that power was no longer confined by time or place, but was available anywhere to those who saw God in him. That is why the prudently neutral historian Josephus reported at the end of the first century that "those who had in the first place come to love him, did not give up their affection for him . . . and the tribe of the Christians, so called after him, has still to this day, not disappeared."

Such is my picture of the historical Jesus. In his offer of free healing and common eating he announced and created a community that was his *no* to the established hierarchical, patronal patterns of his society. Lest he himself be interpreted as simply the new broker of a new God, he moved on constantly, never settling down. He would not be a mediator, but rather the announcer that no mediator should exist between persons, or between persons and God. He announced, in other words, the unmediated or brokerless Kingdom of God.

One of your critics has suggested that your emphasis on Jesus as a peasant resister in an imperial colony comes out of your own experience of growing up in Ireland under British rule. Is that possible?

Well, it's certainly true of all of us that what we see depends on where we stand when we look. If you are a woman in a male-dominated society, or an African-American in a white-dominated society, for example, you may indeed see realities that others either miss or deny. And in that sense, no doubt I grew up unlikely to see empire as a benign reality. But if so, I'd say that my life experience led me to see something that was really going on with and around Jesus—not to *invent* it.

I grew up among the first generation of post-colonial Irish as the British Empire was beginning to decline. I certainly learned what awful things Britain had done to Ireland—but I also received a classically British education, including texts chosen to prepare British youths to administer the Empire. And while my paternal grandparents were lower class peasant farmers, my maternal grandparents were middle class urban shopkeepers. I repeat: I hope that my background sensitized me to injustice, in the first century as well as the twentieth, but I deny that it moved me to invent first-century evidence that wasn't really there.

The Jesus you reconstruct—moving among peasants to rebuild society "from the bottom up"—sounds a lot like the Jesus of Latin America's liberation theology.

If so, it's not because I am a student of liberation theology. If the historical Jesus fits into the Latin American situation, perhaps it is because that situation actually resembles his.

Think, for example, of Archbishop Oscar Romero. In the late 1970s he became Archbishop of San Salvador, in a land where a tiny wealthy elite controlled politics, economics, and the military while the vast majority lived in peasant poverty. Historically, the Church had identified with the interests of the elite. But Romero, as a good pastor, went out among the people—and the people converted their bishop. He began to speak out forcefully, both against unjust privilege and violence on the political right, and against violence and ideology on the guerrilla left.

Against those who wanted a gospel "so disembodied that it doesn't get involved at all in the world it must save," he insisted that "God is doing *now*" what Christ did *then*:

"shaking off oppressive yokes, bringing joy to hearts, sow-
ing hope." He became the voice for the voiceless: those in
shacks and shanty towns, coffee harvesters, the "disappeared" and tortured. Only the person who is concerned
for the hungry, the naked, the poor, the tortured, he said,
"has God close at hand." Mere charity, he insisted, is not
enough, for it is "a caricature of love to try to cover over
with alms what is lacking in justice." In the words of his
Christmas Eve homily in 1979:

> *We must not seek the child Jesus in the pretty figures of our*
> *Christmas cribs.*
>   *We must seek him among the undernourished children*
> *who have gone to bed tonight without eating, among the*
> *poor newsboys who will sleep covered with newspapers in*
> *doorways.*

Accused by politicians and media of supporting subver-
sion, he denied the charge—"unless the gospel is to be
called subversive, because it does indeed touch the founda-
tions of an order that should not exist, because it is unjust."
    Predictably—and he was aware of the fate awaiting
him—Archbishop Romero was murdered by a death squad
while saying Mass, in Lent, 1980.
    But, like the Jesus story, it didn't end there. When, thir-
teen years later, a group of scholars gathered in Chicago for
a symposium on my historical research, I was moved by the
reflections of Catherine Keller, who teaches in the
Theology School of Drew University. She had recently
returned from El Salvador, where she admitted "that for
the first time in my life the early Christian story became
real for me." There she encountered a grassroots community organized around *eating* (for example, taking food to
university students held in prison, and not fed by the government) and *healing* of bodies and psyches.
    Though the "resurrected Romero" appeared on murals

everywhere, she said, "he appears on a continuum with all the other people's martyrs, male and female, who gave their life for the people—precisely *not* in any grotesque attempt to satisfy God through an atoning sacrifice, but by sharing their lives so fully that the death forces could not tolerate them." She found people living boldly in the face of death—with "zest and high good humor, a delight in the sensuality of terrestrial life, an iridescent hope (not optimism), combining itself with clear critical analysis of history and global politics." In such community, she said, she felt close to what Jesus called the Kingdom of God. Crucifixion and resurrection became present realities for Keller through one Salvadoran woman's sense of the legacy of her mother, who had been abducted, raped, and murdered because of her commitment to justice: "The evil forces were not able to stop what for her had meant life."

Who can hear such a story and not recognize in our own generation the continuing reality and power of the gospel of the Kingdom?

Your picture of the historical Jesus—how does it fit with Church teachings about him?

The question deserves a book of its own! But let me try to put it in a nutshell. Our term "Jesus Christ" sums up the issue. "Jesus" is the historical person; "Christ" affirms who he is for believers. "Christ" comes from a Greek word which means the same as "Messiah" which comes from a Hebrew word. Both mean "the Anointed One" and they sum up Jewish hopes for a God-sent deliverer. "Jesus Christ" is thus not a first and last name, but a name and a title: "Jesus who is the Christ (Messiah)."

Christian faith is always *faith in the historical Jesus as a manifestation of God to us*. Faith is more than historical reconstruction. Someone might think that I had done a good job of scholarly research and say, "That's all very interesting, about Jesus' itinerancy, his challenge to conventional lifestyle, his open meals . . . but nothing I want to organize *my* life around." It's possible to accept the historical facts but to conclude that Jesus was utopian, or mistaken, or flaky, or whatever. Christian *faith* means finding in the picture of the historical Jesus the power and wisdom of God—and then getting serious about its implications for *our* lives, now.

So faith goes beyond the historical *facts* to wrestle with their *meanings*. But faith cannot ignore or bypass the historical facts. What we believe in by faith is the ultimate meaning of what we know by history. But the historical reconstruction informs the faith. If I find, for instance, that the historical Jesus called people into an "unbrokered" relationship with God, I can't very well put my faith in a Christ who is conceived as the sole mediator between God and humanity. If I find a Jesus who acts out the Kingdom around an open table, I can't invest faith in a Christ who is a social or moral segregationist. "Christ" is more than "Jesus," but not less. In short, if my faith in Christ doesn't interpret at the deepest level what I know about the historical Jesus, I'd better reexamine my faith.

Your books make a lot of sense to me, but I have a problem of sitting through church on Sunday and having lots of questions in my mind about what is going on. I find meaning in being part of the Church, but I also don't know what to make of this new way of understanding Jesus. What am I to do?

Well, some elements in any parish may, in fact, need to be reformed. If, for example, one has an authoritarian pastor, then I would say that is unacceptable. I don't see how there can be argument on that point—Jesus makes it plain that masters are to behave like servants. He makes it plain that you can't be a Christian leader by playing boss. So I wouldn't have any patience with that kind of parish life.

As for the Eucharist, I would say that its meaning is that God and Jesus are present to us, as food, but *equally* for all. Nobody gets a bigger host or more wine than another, even in this ritualized form of a meal. The question is whether our present forms show some continuity with what Jesus was doing in his ministry. For me the sense of equality before God in the community of faith is absolutely central. Without that sense of equality the tie between Jesus' meal practice and the Eucharist is broken. So the critical question is: In our current forms of church life does our celebration reflect or break continuity with Jesus?

By the way, what I say about Eucharistic liturgy I would say also about a Pentecostal celebration. Take, for example, speaking in tongues. If worshipers draw the conclusion that those who speak in tongues are superior to others, that breaks the continuity with Jesus. If they draw the conclusion that the Spirit is equally available to all and is unpredictable, then they are in continuity with Jesus. That's the question about our forms, not whether they are exactly what Jesus did, but whether or not they are consistent with his basic emphasis. I would also ask: Is what we do in worship a once-a-week escape from the world, or is it a beachhead for Jesus' incursion into the world?

Will you say something about your own spiritual life and connection with the Church?

I spent twenty years of my life in a monastic order with four or five hours a day of formal prayer. I left the priesthood in 1969 because, as I indicated earlier, I wanted to marry, and also because of an acute distaste for how the Roman Catholic hierarchy operated. My intelligence and my conscience were repeatedly insulted, and I was constantly in trouble for saying out loud what I had found in my research. I wanted to get away from that. I didn't want to have to constantly argue with the hierarchy and let them set my agenda. So I basically decided, "You leave me alone, and I'll leave you alone." But I have always considered myself a member of the Roman Catholic tradition and the Roman Catholic community. I just need a certain therapeutic distance, a certain strategic separation from the Roman Catholic hierarchy. But I would also say that I can no longer distinguish between prayer and study. If the function of prayer is to allow God to get at you, then scholarship is where that now happens for me. Someone asked me in an interview what I would do differently if I had my life to live over. I would do it exactly the same way over again, because I like the way it came out. If I had to do it all over again, I would spend twenty years in a monastery. If I had to do it all over again, I would also leave that monastery.

If you could wave a magic wand over the Church to produce any change that you wanted, what would it be?

I would reverse the entire method of decision making so that issues would be decided from the bottom up. I would want a church where there were *no magic wands* that anybody could wave from the top down. You know, if the Pope would say tomorrow that women can now be priests, I'm not at all sure that would be a good idea—simply because it would be pronounced from the top down. The world has changed from an authoritarian, hierarchical style of public life, and the Church never did change. Even the *language* has not changed since the time of the Roman Empire. When I was a monk in Rome, the allowance that I received for my living expenses was called by a Latin term that came down from what the Romans paid the slaves. What I think we need in the Church is to generate maximum discussion about important issues, like birth control and abortion, instead of telling everyone what to think and do. So if I could wave a magic wand, I would get rid of the waving of magic wands.

My final query is a question about a question. If you got to ask Jesus one question, what would that question be?

One of the people who wrote to me did so under the guise of two letters to Jesus. I cannot think of any better questions to ask Jesus than the ones formulated in those letters. Here is a combined extract:

Dear Jesus,

A small group of us have just begun reading your biography by Dominic Crossan. At the rate we have started, we may never finish even his shorter version. One of the things Mr. Crossan does at the very beginning of this book is talk about your world, the world into which you came. His point, I believe, is that if we are to truly understand you we must try to know your context. (I've cheated and read ahead.) . . .

So very many of the issues seem different. I am part of a group that has political power, you were not. I can foster changes in the laws, you could not. I can help them be fairer or less fair, you could not. . . . I know it's imperfect, but I just can't believe you would have walked away from it. It can help people. Good laws, at their very best, are loving. I thought that was what we were all about. . . .

You seemed more than other great religious leaders to care about the lives of actual people, their pain, illness, grief. If we are to live life lovingly, does that not mean we are to use whatever loving tools we have to open the possibility for others? Does that hold for you as well? . . .

Is it possible that the words you were speaking then are

irrelevant to me in my situation? I cannot believe the intent, to be loving to one another, is outdated. . . .

I am increasingly afraid that in many cases you said exactly what you meant, instead of the watered-down version I have often chosen to swallow. Dr. Crossan has about convinced me that when you said, "Blessed are the poor, for they are the only ones who do not have dirty hands," you meant exactly that. This is a message which is neither comfortable nor palatable, and it is just one of many. What makes all this far worse is that Dr. Crossan is one of your followers who, at least in terms of biology, sees you as a man, conforming to the laws of physics as other men. Far from decreasing your status, in my mind at least, it increases it. It means that without any help from an E.T., an individual can live as you did and perhaps even die as you died. These are not comfortable thoughts. . . .

I have decided to ask three questions: (1) What were you advocating as a life program in your time and place? (Crossan is a great help in this, some of the first I have received that seems sensible); (2) How does that message translate to me and to today? (Crossan is helpful here, but he could do more in this respect . . . another book perhaps?); (3) When I can answer number two above, passably well, I will ask: Do I agree with you? Can I do it—or, perhaps more honestly, am I willing to?

I have a terrible feeling that I may find answers most uncomfortable. However, I believe I would rather say, "I think you were wrong" (however blasphemous that may sound) than try to fudge it all by maintaining you didn't actually say it. I also think I will be more at peace with myself (although not very) saying, "I can't do as you ask" than I will be if I am a hypocrite about what it is that you have asked. It seems to me that the weak fared better than the hypocrites when you were teaching. . . .

A woman from Ohio

JOHN DOMINIC CROSSAN is emeritus professor of biblical studies at DePaul University in Chicago. He is the best-selling author of many books, including *The Historical Jesus*, *Jesus: A Revolutionary Biography*, *The Essential Jesus*, and *Who Killed Jesus?* His most recent book, *The Birth of Christianity*, was chosen by *Publisher's Weekly* as one of the ten best religious books of 1998.

RICHARD G. WATTS recently retired as pastor of New Covenant Community in Normal, Illinois, a union congregation of the Christian Church (Disciples of Christ), the Presbyterian Church (U.S.A.), and the United Church of Christ.